LET GO

Contents

ABOUT THE AUTHOR

Srinivas Gokulnath (Srini) is a passionate ultra-cyclist, and was the first Indian to complete Race Across America (RAAM) in the Solo category by cycling 3000 miles (around 5000 km) in 11 days, 18 hours and 45 minutes in the 2017 edition of the race. He was also the first solo Indian cyclist to complete Race Around Austria (RAA) in 2018, cycling 2200 km in 5 days, 10 hours and 8 minutes. In 2014, he cycled 4000 km from the northern tip to the southern tip of India, for which he holds the national record for completion in 16 days.

An aerospace medicine specialist by profession, Srini has been serving with the Indian Armed Forces for 16 years, with vast experience in military medicine, aerospace medicine and high-altitude warfare. He has served in high altitude areas such as the Siachen Glacier, in deserts and high conflict zones. Srini has also led teams in different military exercises. He is a TEDX speaker and a motivational speaker.

Srini is happily married to Prafulla Srinivas, a paediatrician by profession, and has a 7-year-old son Rohan. They live in Bangalore, India.

Presently he is serving as a UN Peacekeeper from India at the UNMISS (United Nations Mission in South Sudan) heading two Aero-medical Evacuation teams (AMET).

ABOUT THE BOOK

Srini is an ordinary guy who aspires to explore himself through his passion in Ultra-cycling. His journey to excel by being the first Indian to finish the World's toughest Ultra-endurance bicycling race called Race Across America (RAAM) is transformational.

Srini finding his interest in Ultra-cycling, setting higher goals to excel, failing miserably and bouncing back to understand the importance of attributes such as self-belief, a strong desire, making use of failure, accepting challenges, the power of humility, spirit of team work and letting go of the ordinary are highlighted through his life experiences.

This book intends to focus on the key transformation that occurs in an individual as they follow their passion. It talks about the value of emotions, beliefs, attitudes and other psychosocial aspects that are required to successfully finish the world's toughest ultra-cycling race, Race Across America (RAAM).   The purpose of this book is to emphasize how the concept of "Let Go" can have a profound impact on our lives as seen through Srini's journey.

ACKNOWLEDGEMENTS

I'm extraordinarily grateful to my wife Prafulla, my son Rohan, and to my family members who have supported me since I decided to follow my passion in ultra-cycling. They have all endured and sacrificed many years of their time and energies.

I'm also grateful to my friends from school, coaching class, medical college, and certainly my cycling community for their support in my undertaking of ultra-cycling and all the challenges that come with it.

I'm ever grateful to my incredible crew members who have been selfless in their service for me to reach the finish line of Race Across America (RAAM). Listing them here:

Kishore Gopalakrishna, USA	Dhanashekar S, IND
Shreyash K Gowda, IND	Gyanendra Sharma, IND
Venkatesha Shivarama, IND	Niranjan Upasani, IND
Sudhakara Narasegowda, IND	Chris O Keefe, USA
Yin Shortland, USA	Alberto Blanco, USA
Supratim Pal, IND	Sundaram Narayanan, IND
Maika, USA	Rutvik Khare, IND
Chris Davies, USA	Martin Gruebele, USA
Anthony Shortland, USA	

ACKNOWLEDGEMENTS

I'm thankful to Nashik cycling club, Bangalore Bicycle Club, Pune Cycling club and the race Director of Deccan Cliffhanger for all the support they offered to do Race Across America (RAAM).

I'm also very thankful to my friends who have helped me in the creation of this book, without their kind support, this project would not have seen the light of the day. They helped me to create and publish this book. Listing them here:

Sudhakara Narasegowda, IND   Kristi H Ashwill, USA

Subhash Lagali, IND   GIRI MEDIA TEAM, IND

I'm proud and thankful to be serving in Indian Armed Forces, from which I have received great support, especially in lending me the required space and time to follow my passion in ultra-cycling.

DEDICATIONS

This book is dedicated to,

My wife Prafulla Srinivas and our son, Rohan Srinivas

My Parents (Mrs Radha Gokulnath & Mr M Gokulnath)

My In-laws (Mrs Jaya Srinivas & Mr B M Srinivas)

My Support Crew members in all my Ultra-cycling races but especially to who made RAAM a success, listing them out here:

Kishore Gopalakrishna, USA	Dhanashekar S, IND
Shreyash K Gowda, IND	Gyanendra Sharma, IND
Venkatesha Shivarama, IND	Niranjan Upasani, IND
Sudhakara Narasegowda, IND	Chris O Keefe, USA
Yin Shortland, USA	Alberto Blanco, USA
Supratim Pal, IND	Sundaram Narayanan, IND
Maika, USA	Rutvik Khare, IND

My school friends, coaching class friends and my friends from 1998 batch of Dr B R Ambedkar Medical College, Bangalore.

My friends and colleagues in the Armed Forces.

My friend Late Dave Tanner from Bloomington, Indiana.

Without their selfless and relentless support, I would not have been able to accomplish the feat to be the first Indian to finish Race Across America.

1. THE GOOD HURT

Srini in Utah, Race Across America 2017

"What the hell is this guy doing? I don't think he is going to make it to the finish line, or to Durango even! Have I signed up for a race where the racer is not prepared enough? He is not doing great; if he continues like this, I'm going to pack up my bags and go back" said Chris to Dave. The "guy" in question was me, Srini, and unbeknown to them, I had overheard their conversation.

This was happening at 1:00 PM on 16th June 2017 amidst the scorching heat of the Navajo Nation. An iconic symbol of the American West, the high desert of Monument Valley, Utah was indeed the ideal setting for an adventure.

Chris O'Keefe from California was the Crew Chief, the leader of Team Srini. I was a solo rider on a mission to ride a bicycle across the vast country of the United States of America, I had 11 crew members to support me. Team Srini was in a race, really?

So, what was this all about?

It was just a bicycle race called Race Across America (RAAM). Well, the word "just" here just does not do justice to this race which involves cycling from the West Coast to the East Coast of the fourth largest country in the world by area, the United States of America. The distance involved is around 5000 km or 3000 miles, in a given time of 12 days. "Cycling 5000 km in 12 days, you must be kidding," is probably what you would think, but yes, this crazy Ultra-endurance event has been conducted every year since 1982 and is one of the toughest Ultra Cycling races in the world. It begins at Oceanside, courses through the dry deserts of California and Arizona, crosses the Rocky Mountains of Colorado, stretches through the plains of Kansas, crosses the Appalachian mountain ranges, and finally ends at the dockside in Annapolis, Maryland.

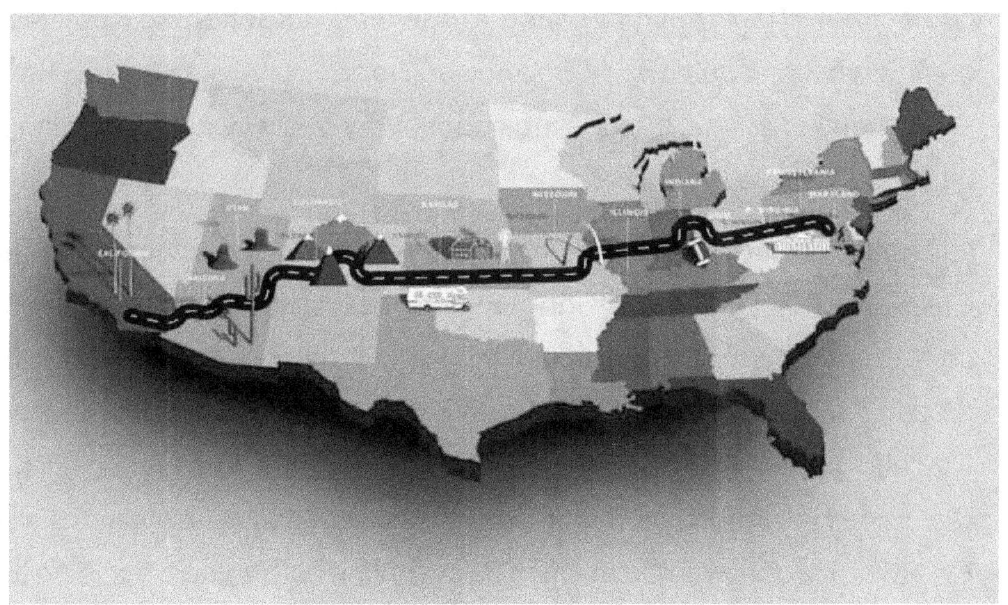

The Race route of RAAM starts from West Coast moves to East Coast of USA

There are currently 7.8 billion people in the world. In the recorded history of humankind, approximately over 550 people have been to space, around 5000 have climbed Mount Everest, 1 million have completed the Ironman triathlon, and around 2000 have crossed the English Channel. In the thirty-eight years of RAAM's history, there have been only 346 official finishers to date, which makes the race one of the toughest of its kind. It is a time trial race, and once started the clock does not stop for any reason for the next 288 hours or 12 days. The 3000-mile race route is divided into fifty-five time-stations from start to finish, and spanning three time zones, three mountain passes, four rivers and extremes of temperatures. The race is interesting, to say the very least. Going back to the conversation which I overheard between Chris and Dave, 20 miles before Time Station (TS) 12 at Mexican Hat, Utah. It was the third day of the race and Chris had officially lost all hope on me. I could hear them only because Chris had forgotten to mute his communication equipment (Terranos or Cardos) when he was talking to Dave, venting out his true feelings about how badly I was performing in this brutal bicycle race across...

I had known Chris for over a year and had requested him to be the Crew Chief to lead Team Srini towards the finish line. Chris, having completed this race successfully in the past as a solo rider, knew the race like the back of his hand. Dave Tanner, who had done the same, was also crewing for another solo rider participating in this race. Dave, Chris and I had become friends through our respective associations with RAAM - I, for one, wanted to finish RAAM in the solo category and be the first Indian to do it. Along with Chris and the other crew members, we had worked together towards this aim, strategizing about the race execution well in advance, almost for 11 months. Now, after cycling 800 miles in 72 hours, I was shaken and shattered by the knowledge that my Crew Chief had lost faith in me. It wasn't something I had expected. I trusted Chris and thought he trusted me, too.

At this point, I was definitely struggling to ride strong and had been overtaken by nearly every other participant in the race. I was trying my best to figure out why I was riding that poorly. Chris and the crew were also trying their best to help me ride faster. Day 2 had started out quite badly on my way to TS (Time Station) 9 at Flagstaff, Arizona. This time station was one of the hardest parts of the race and I struggled to make it due to dehydration. I knew I was not doing great - I had lost around 8 hours of time when I reached the state of Utah.

Unable to digest this information and feeling betrayed, I still tried to continue cycling. But Chris' words had knocked me out completely. In the next few minutes, I got off the bicycle and stopped the race. Fired up and upset, I requested all my crew members, both the day and the night crew, to pull over to the wide shoulder of the road. The crew members were unaware of this abrupt stoppage by their racer. This was the first time they had seen me do this and they were puzzled. What was running through Srini's mind? The Sun was right above their heads, and the mountains of Monument Valley were fiercely shining red in the background.

Srini riding in Utah. On the far-left the Day crew waits for the unplanned team meeting called for by Srini. Day 3 of the race, 20 miles before Monument Valley

So now on that wide shoulder, the entire team had assembled - me, eleven crew members, three minivans and two bicycles. I told them that I wanted to discuss something important with my core crew members, specifically Chris, Prafulla Srinivas (my wife), Sudhakara Narasegowda (Sudha), Yin Shortland and Venkatesh Shivarama (Venky). I admitted I was not doing well and had lost a lot of time, that I would not make it to the next time station, which was Durango, Colorado in the stipulated time, and that I still did not want to give up. What I wanted, was to skip the scheduled sleep break and ride non-stop to Durango to make up for the loss. The crew members could see the hard-core, intense Srini, talking to them as if this was the end of the world. This was it! The meeting was like an intense operational briefing right in the war zone.

After stating this, I requested each of the crew members to give their honest opinion on how they thought we should deal with the ongoing crisis. Sudha, my school friend says "Let's stick to the plan Srini, take the next sleep break and then ride strong". Yin, Chris' sister-in-law, was particularly assertive, without an iota of doubt, she says, "Stick to the plan, don't skip the sleep break". All the other crew members, Prafulla and Venky included, were also of the same opinion. But when it was Chris' turn to speak, he said, "I'm Ok for you to ride without a sleep break, that's your choice. The numbers don't look bright but magic could happen." Chris knew I was at the end of my rope and Chris was almost willing to compromise the main plan or strategy. In that moment, Yin and the others were stronger than him and insisted we stick to the plan and the next sleep break.

Was this the "Jesus moment" of our adventure?

A lot was running through my mind. I was hurt, broken and devastated, but I wanted to stay alive in the race. I was not doing well; I sought support and wanted to take control of the situation through complete submission to my crew. Chris, though brutally honest, had channelled that honesty into his phone call with Dave instead of being upfront with me.

The moment of hurt in the Wild West brought a lot of transparency to the team. We were exposed, stripped bare and exceptionally vulnerable in the heat of Monument Valley. It felt something like a company going bankrupt, or a relationship falling apart. It was definitely a strong realization for me - this race was crumbling down. Would I succumb to this hard fact, or would I ride forward to the East Coast with hope, despite this demoralized state of my race?

It was the "Do or Die" moment for Team Srini.

2. CHILD IN YOU

Devasandra, Bangalore

Devasandra is a small area in the big city of Bangalore. Many Bangaloreans didn't even know it existed until the coming of the International Tech Park (ITPL) in 1994, with which came a boom of petrol stations, apartments, educational institutions and city buses - I was unknowingly witnessing this gradual change in my hometown.

Back in my childhood, however, Devasandra was home to rural living, with paddy fields, guava orchards, vineyards, lakes, temples, village festivals and so on. Life just a few kilometres away was more urbanised and modern. This was the village I lived in from the fifteenth day of my existence, although I was born on November 8th, 1980 at a Government hospital in my mother's village of Tirupattur in Tamil Nadu.

Srini's family pic at Bangalore in 1987, L-R: six-year-old Srini, Srini's father, mother and three-year-old brother Sai Kumar

Growing up, I'd see the boys of my village playing games like cricket, while the girls would play cooking games. I, however, enjoyed both and was never bored. The most boring thing for me was being at home. Though full of adventure, curiosity, and life, I recall being constantly stressed out by the financial issues at home, my Parents quarrels, and my schooling. In fourth grade, my math teacher gave us some problems and insisted we solved them quickly. Without a clue as to the method of solving such a problem, I succumbed to the pressure and checked the answer from the back of the book (which was not allowed). Eventually, she realised what I had done, and I had lied and said I had used my own methods, she caned my knuckles in front of my classmates. I accepted that I had cheated. Yet, she continued humiliating me and never made an effort to actually teach me the method to arrive at the solution. I was deeply upset by this. The only way to find happiness back then was to play outdoors until I was exhausted. My younger brother, Sai Kumar, was three years younger than me and would tag along wherever I went.

Learning to ride a bicycle gave me the wings to explore. It was on my father's Raleigh bicycle (often used by milkmen) that I taught myself how to ride at the age of six. The bicycle was big for a six-year-old, but I found different ways to ride and progress. I started with my feet on the pedals and legs inside the triangular frame, then progressed to sitting on the top tube of the frame, then finally sitting on the saddle when I was tall enough. Finding balance at each stage was a huge accomplishment. On that bicycle, I explored many places, routes, villages, and also used it for my commute to school. It was at the age of 14 years that I insisted that my parents get me a new mountain bicycle, though it was tough to expect them to shell out Rs 2800 (approx. 40 USD). While I also loved to play Cricket and wanted to join the ITI cricket club, my parents could not afford the joining fee for it either. My father was the only breadwinner and our entire family relied on his bare-minimum monthly salary, which barely covered our basic necessities of food, shelter, and education. I saw my parents struggle to make ends meet. The four of us lived in a house that had an asbestos roof, one bedroom, hall, and a kitchen. Many times, they would borrow money from our neighbours with huge interest rates. It was all about survival. Asking for a bicycle was unjustified. Yet, my mother found ways to save some money every month. After six months, I was gifted with my dream bicycle.

As I reached the tenth grade, schooling was stressful except for the sports and games, and the friends I made through them. I did not fare well in the tenth grade Board Exams and was finding it difficult to gain admission into the Science category of any school. It was then that it struck me how much I had neglected my studies. Finally, when I did get accepted by a school, I valued that opportunity and vowed to do my best. I was attentive; I made my studies a priority. I felt I could excel if I did this and sought to understand logic. In spite of a hiccup during the final exams, as I had prepared for Physics on the day of the Mathematics exam, I fared well in the 11th Grade, scoring 90 out of 100 in Physics and 68 out of 100 in Mathematics.

Things were taken up a notch in the 12th Grade as our scores would be the deciding factor in gaining admission into professional college courses. The competition is always high in India, so I joined coaching classes. The fees for this was an added financial stressor for my parents. While joining, one of the teachers asked about my 10th Grade scores. When I disclosed the numbers, he bluntly said, "Do you think you can match up to the brilliant students at our centre? Well, I really don't think you can, because as per my experience students with such poor performance in Science and Maths in 10th grade will never excel in the 12th grade. Your parents are unnecessarily wasting money on you."

I was upset by this and it sparked a burning fire in me to work hard and succeed.

The Coaching Centre was 1 mile/1.6 km away, and my school 6 mile/10 km away from home. I had a set routine - waking up by 4 am to study till 8 am, going to the temple, then to school and back by 4 pm, and tuitions till 8 pm. This continued for 12 months. Nearly all of my commute was on my bicycle.

My favourite subjects were Chemistry, Mathematics, Biology and Physics, strictly in that order. With a laser-like focus and a fair amount of guilt over-burdening my parents financially, I wanted to make the best of this opportunity. My performance was gradually improving - I, who until the 11th grade did not even know how to divide a fraction, was now making quick progress in learning concepts, and even topping some of the weekly tests! By the end of 10 months of coaching, my tuition teachers were giving me positive feedback on my progress, which motivated me further as I was breaking the preconceived notions they had once held about me. I finally felt seen; like I existed.

Sudhakara (Sudha) and Kiran Bhongale were my closest friends, who were as enthusiastic about learning and on the same wavelength as me. They, too, were constantly working hard to excel in the Grade 12 Boards Exams. Our efforts eventually paid off and we were each accepted into professional courses of our choice - I joined the Dr BR Ambedkar Medical College in Bangalore, while Sudha and Kiran were accepted into an Engineering College and a Medical School in Bangalore as well, respectively. We got busy in our own ways.

Med School

At medical school, I felt like a wide-eyed amateur, very guarded, timid, and inexpressive, but a hard worker. I really wanted to do justice towards my course. It was a whole new world of academics, interpersonal connections, extracurricular activities. I admit, the five years of medical school were not easy. I had several ups and downs. It was also when I had to break out of my shell with regards to interacting comfortably with girls. In fact, I even developed a crush on one of my college-mates and was heartbroken when, after almost two years of unprofessed feelings, she introduced me to her boyfriend! Fortunately, I had plenty else going on, from playing sports in the mornings and attending theory and laboratory classes for the remainder of the day. Outdoor activities, sports and games were my greatest outlet.

The final phase of the Med school had a tinge of tragedy to it. Immediately after my final year exams in Med School, I started to work part-time at a medical transcription company. Tragically, within the next 15 days my father, who was working in a steel factory lost his job. Sai Kumar had just joined an Engineering college. The news of my father losing his job was revealed to me when I called my mother to tell her I'd received my first pay check. Instead of her being happy, she shared the sad news. I made up my mind to take charge of the family's finances and my brother's education. The part time job was now indispensable, and I picked up additional night duty at a Hospital. So, a typical day looked like this:

8 am to 2 pm:	Internship at the Medical college/Hospital
2 pm to 5 pm:	Teaching 'Language of Medicine' at the Medical Transcription company
8 pm to 8 am:	Work as a Duty Doctor at the Hospital

I'd squeeze in some sleep if there were no patients at the Emergency department of the Hospital at night. Then, go home for two hours after teaching Medical transcription, to take a shower, change my clothes and

18

pack a meal. This continued for two years. I was now a workaholic who experienced sleep disorders such as somnambulism, sleep-talking and dozing off at traffic signals on the motorcycle. It was a dangerous lifestyle. I happened to disclose my struggles to Nagendra Prasad, a senior from Med School, who suggested I apply for a job in the Army Medical Corps, as that would help stabilize our financial problems.

Joining Armed Forces

Pictures taken at the Siachen Glacier while Srini served with the Tibetan troops in 2007

In 2005, I joined the Indian Army as a Medical Officer posted at the Military Hospital in Belgaum. The basic military training we had to undergo there involved, physical training to build fitness, combat survival and weapons training, an understanding of the structure, laws and etiquette of the Armed Forces, and military medicine. After this, I was posted to an Infantry regiment in Jammu and Kashmir. I was a reformed person with self-confidence and pride in my Uniformed service. I volunteered to serve with the Special Forces at the Siachen Glacier, the world's highest altitude battlefield.

From November 2006 to March 2007, I served at the Siachen Glacier at 17000 ft altitude, where the temperature varied between +10 °C and - 58 °C, with frequent avalanches and numerous crevasses all around our camp. Once, a 50-year old soldier with six gangrenous toes was handed over to me by my predecessor, who stated that gangrene was in the healing stage and that the wounds were minor. However, as I examined the cold injuries, it looked bad and did not seem treatable in that isolated post. Since the soldier held an important position and his presence was very vital for the morale of the troops, his senior colleagues insisted on retaining him at the post. I had to rise up to the challenge, knowing it was going to be risky as our set-up was only meant to cater to medical emergencies and to offer primary treatment at the post. The most important requirement for swift wound healing is regular sterile dressing. If due concern is given to the minutest details of maintaining an aseptic environment, then the battle is half won – so, for a lack of better means, I decided to use a pressure cooker to sterilize the surgical instruments and dressing. Thankfully, it turned out to be a useful hack and by the end of three weeks, there were signs of healing in all the six toes. I continued to dress the wounds for another three weeks and after 98 days of relentless efforts, they were completely healed. Incidents such as these helped me build confidence to treat cold injuries and other high-altitude illnesses.

Serving at the glacier with Tibetan troops, I tried my best to build a rapport with them, accompanying them on half-link treks and thus getting better at snow-craft. I also assisted in retrieving the dry rations which were para dropped into the snow bowls. All these patrols were rife with close encounters with avalanches, crevasses, snow blizzards and snow-scooter accidents. Yet, my skills were improving. By the end of the tenure, I was extremely strong.

By the end of March 2007, I moved out of the Siachen glacier to another high-altitude post in Kashmir at 14000 ft. It snows heavily in winter and remains cut off from the rest of the world for almost 6 months. Yet, with my experience at the glacier I was now able to adjust to the isolation and the rugged terrain much faster, and went on regular foot patrols to understand the area.

The snow continued to fall for over three weeks. By the end of Dec 2007, there was an urgent need to evacuate a section of troops. They had run out of food and fuel and were also facing the threat of an avalanche. I volunteered to be a part of the rescue party. The weather was getting worse with snow blizzards, gushing winds and heavy snowfall with zero visibility. We were in constant radio communication with the troops. The five porters with the rescue party moved ahead and descended down the hill to meet up with the incoming troops, and informed us that they were now climbing and needed some rope for assistance. There was a loud bang after this message, and the radio communication with the troops was lost. There was complete silence. It took us a while to realise that an avalanche had engulfed the troops and porters. There were fifteen people caught in the avalanche. The inaction and delay in decision-making made me restless, so I went ahead towards the site of the avalanche. Crawling to avoid triggering another avalanche, I was followed by two soldiers called Lokender and Koshty. We crawled for three hours to reach the avalanche site. I spotted a black glove embedded in the snow. That's how we pulled out soldier Ankush Jadhav, who was conscious but gasping for breath. I revived him with a

Hydrocortisone injection. This was repeated with Mukesh Chouragade who was also in a bad condition. In the meantime, the rest of the rescue party had made its way to the avalanche site where another soldier retrieved. After a while of basic life support, he was declared dead.

There were thirteen people still untraceable. I gave Ankush and Mukesh another shot of hydrocortisone each and some puffs from the Asthalin inhaler to ready them for the trip back to the post. It was time to ascend towards the base. Ankush and Mukesh's survival on the journey to the post was my responsibility. We finally reached the base at 3:30 A.M. after over 24 hours of this gruelling, emotionally-charged experience. On opening the soldiers' gloves and clothes, I found that all digits on their hands and feet were frostbitten, as were their noses. Warm intravenous fluids were administered and all the wounds were dressed with sterile dressings.

This base was a shelter made of stones. It was not a hospital, just a place to stay which had now been converted into a room for Ankush and Mukesh. I did not have medical assistants. The bad weather continued for almost three weeks. I tended to the soldiers' wounds and health. The treatment continued for 52 days after which both were air-evacuated to a hospital. Both Ankush and Mukesh showed great improvement during their time with me. Ankush and Mukesh contacted me after 6 months when I had moved to Hyderabad. I was very happy to hear that their fingers and toes were saved for both.

I was also extensively involved in the retrieval of the 13 bodies from the avalanche site and arranged for evacuation down to the rear. Retrieving the dead from an avalanche site after almost fifty days was a massive exercise in itself. The search for the dead was like looking for a needle in haystack, physically very demanding. Around twenty men would get down to the valley bowl and dig almost 15 feet of snow around an area of almost two football fields. I accompanied them every single day for almost a month. The moment we spotted the dead body, we were ironically happy, isn't that strange, that you spot the dead and you are happy, but that's how it is, finding a dead body gave a meaningful end or solace to us and to the family members of the bereaved soldier who are thousands of miles away from the site of the incident. The retrieved bodies were deformed and frozen in several shapes and to sledge them vertically up on a slope at an altitude of 15000 ft for almost 1.3 mile/2 km was a demanding task and required a minimum of six men for carrying on body to a safe place near the post. It took almost two months to retrieve the 13 bodies, even though we worked for 13 hours each day in the snow. I did my best to lend a helping hand in the process whether it is ploughing the snow or pulling the sledge and also loading the bodies in the helicopter.

Soldiers Mukesh Chourgade and Ankush Jadhav

3. FOUND IT…

Back to Bangalore

I served in harsh environments for four years. During my field tenure with the Armed Forces, I applied for and got the opportunity to join a post-graduation programme in Aerospace Medicine. I joined Armed forces as a medical officer in Short service commission for five years. In the next two years, I passed an interview to become a permanent commissioned officer. With four years of service, I was eligible to appear for an entrance examination to do post-graduation. I could clear that exam and opt Aerospace medicine for specialization. I would be in Bangalore from 2009 to 2012. This was a turning point in my life. The city of Bangalore, being my hometown, was always special and has a very active bicycling community. Bicycles are widely used for several reasons here - to commute, to race, for leisure, to tour and for fitness. Hope was sparked in getting back in touch with my old passion.

I had once thought that cycling 12 miles/20 km was a big deal. Now I was seeing cyclists riding hundreds of kilometres. I wanted to push my maximum distance to 30 mile/50 kms and then to 63 miles/100 kms, so I started using my single-speed bicycle for my commute. I made an effort to get in touch with various bicycle groups, one of which was the Go Green Cycling Club. From there, I got linked to various bicycle groups, teams, races, and eventually stumbled upon Ultra-distance cycling. My passion for cycling grew each day. I was enthusiastic to explore more, meet more people in the community, and listen to their cycling stories.

I befriended more people within the cycling community, and one such friend was Vijay, who insisted I upgrade to a good road bicycle. The price of these cycles left me shocked, and I decided to not upgrade. Yet one fine day, Vijay, being the good friend that he is, took me to a bicycle shop and bought me a road bike. He told me to pay him back whenever I gathered funds. I was very thankful to him as I never imagined that I would lay hands on a road bike. Now equipped with a Giant Trinity TCR 3, aluminium frame with Shimano Tiagra Groupset, I wasted no time getting used to the bicycle. I felt obliged to do justice to this prized possession. Soon, I was spending my weekends riding distances of 90 miles/150 kms and going on long touring rides with cycling friends to places like Ooty, Coorg, Yercaud, and Hyderabad-- all on our bicycles. It wasn't long before I was known in the bicycle communities as "the cyclist who goes on long rides."

Pictures of Srini's cycling days in Bangalore from 2009-2012

The Bums on The Saddle (BOTS) bicycle shop in Jayanagar once hosted an Indian rider who was preparing to participate in the Race Across America (RAAM) 2010. As part of his presentation, Bicycle Dreams (the most famous documentary on RAAM) was being screened. This film by Stephen Auerbach specifically captures some intense moments of the 2005 edition of the race, while also showcasing the scenic route and inspirational words from the participating riders and coaches. I was truly amazed by the challenges and the pride of finishing such a race, and was already fantasizing about completing it someday. That was when I started following RAAM.

Srini with Prafulla in 2011 in Bangalore

This was also around the time that I formed an amateur cycling team. The four of us would train together, clocking 25 miles/40 kms a day, four days each week, and participate in the monthly Bangalore Bicycle Championships, which consisted of both road races and cross-country races held on the outskirts of the city. The road races were usually 50 -60 miles (80-110 km) long and our team's performance helped us understand the scope for improvement, if we desired to be on the podium. We trained together for almost a year, but gradually the team began to disintegrate.

Simultaneously, I got busy with post- graduation and also decided it was time to get married. Through a Matrimonial website, I met Prafulla, who was pursuing her post-graduation in Paediatrics in Bangalore. We started to hang out and get to know each other - she was a realist while I was always in the virtual world. She was very understanding of my passion for cycling and never had any issues with it. After nearly one year of courtship we both agreed to marry, and got our parents involved. By this time, cycling had taken a back seat. After my post-graduation, I was posted to Jammu and Kashmir as a flight surgeon and was to report by July 2012.

I found my passion in Ultra-cycling in Bangalore, all thanks to the city's lovely cycling community. I now had two major goals:

To ride from the Northern tip to the Southern tip of India

To complete RAAM in the solo category before I turned 40.

4. JOURNEY ACROSS TIPS

Now I wasn't completely happy with this posting as I realised there wouldn't be opportunities to pedal like I had in Bangalore. This new posting to Srinagar was at a 5000 ft altitude, with snowy winters and mountains all around. This place had a peripheral road of about 2 miles/3.3 km and that was all the area I had to cycle outdoors, as moving out of the Garrison was restricted due to security concerns. I was forced to make peace with the situation and started training for 150-180 miles (250-300 km) a week.

Prafulla and I were blessed with a baby boy, Rohan on 29 December 2013. Everyone in the family felt that the cycling would come to a halt, but it was on the contrary, as Prafulla was very supportive and never restricted me from following my passion in Ultra-cycling.

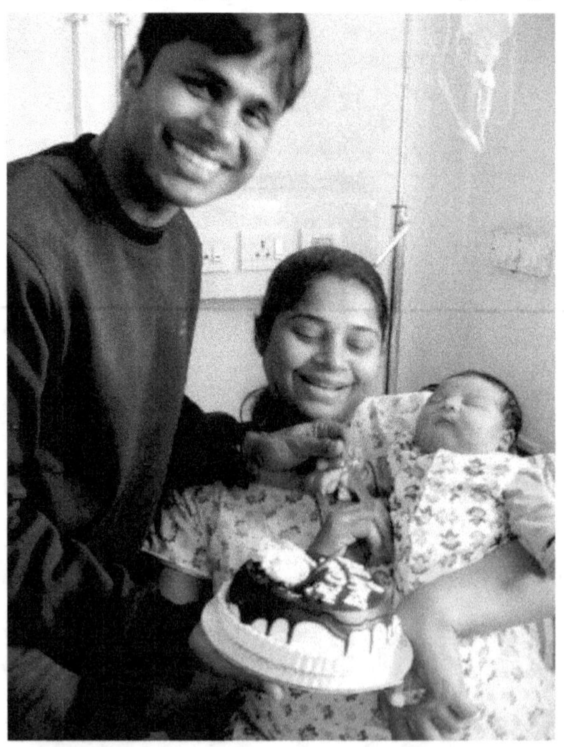

29 December 2013, Bangalore. A new addition to the family. L to R: Srini, Prafulla and Rohan

Life was getting busy. There was not much progress with sponsorship for my undertaking of the Leh-Kanyakumari ride (Northern tip to Southern tip of India). I was looking out for sponsors for bicycles, apparel, a follow vehicle, accommodations and other logistics for undertaking this ride. I knew that it is going to be an expensive affair to ride faster from one tip to another tip of India. This was my first goal: to cycle from the Northernmost to the Southernmost tip of India in the least possible time.

By the end of March 2014, however, I decided I was not going to wait around for sponsors to turn this long-standing dream of mine into a reality. It had been on my mind since 2009, waiting was no longer an option and so I started to plan the ride out on my terms. Sarvesh Kumar, my 24-year old medical assistant at the aviation base was always game for such adventures and was excited to be a part of this expedition. Sarvesh is a soldier from Kanpur working as a medical assistant at the same Aviation base where I was posted. He worked with me in the Medical centre assisting patients with their needs. I found him to be positive and always open for any changes. Sarvesh to me, was like the Robin to Batman. I often used to discuss things that I had in mind in terms of improving the existing health set up, my personal goals, my cycling ambitions and also improving on our efficiency as a team. I used to make sure that all patients who visit the medical centre at the Aviation base would return relieved with their illness as much as possible and would limit unnecessary referrals to the tertiary centre. I was also good at minor surgeries like removing little swellings on the body. Sarvesh was always excited to this way of working, as usually the peripheral Medical centre's refer patients to higher centres. I was treating all kinds of illnesses at this peripheral medical centre with a good nursing team headed by Sarvesh. He gathered all the logistics required for the upcoming cycling adventure. We set September 2014 as the timeframe for our journey, as most mountainous passes along the Leh-Manali road would be open then. Sarvesh was also on the lookout for a support vehicle in Kashmir. Meanwhile, I trained Mariya Dasu, a soldier whom I had met through the Army Personnel's' buddy system, as a bicycle mechanic. He was adept at repairing machinery and I knew he was the man for the job.

Although a Flight Surgeon by training, I had been treating civilian patients from neighbouring villages who sustained injuries due to burns. I gained popularity as the "burns specialist", and was often surprised to see patients with chronic burn injuries from miles away stepping into my tiny clinic. In this pretext, I was able to interact with and establish a good rapport with many civilians in the area.

I trained in the 3.3 km perimeter and simultaneously worked on crew-building and logistics for the race. By June 2014, the plan was taking form. An Air Force officer named R. Anand heard of my plan and contacted me as he was keen on being a part of it. He even offered to pool in resources from his end and ride along the entire route with me. R Anand was posted to an Air Force unit which was 6 miles/10 km away from my post.

In the last week of August 2014, my crew and I finalized our support vehicle, a Mahindra pickup van. Five days before our departure from Srinagar to Leh, we committed a big blunder by fuelling the pickup van with petrol instead of diesel. Before we realised it, the damage to the engine was done. Sarvesh took the van to the mechanic but it was futile; nothing could be done. Panic started to set in. The furious van driver was seeking compensation for the blunder. It felt like we were doomed, but the stage was set. We decided not to give up. Sarvesh not only managed the blunder but also arranged for another pickup van a day before the planned departure. We liaised with the engineering department to modify the vehicle to fit our needs - it had to be compartmentalized into two, with the upper deck for logistics and a lower deck for the crew to sleep. It would also need to carry spare bikes, accessories, and our logistics. Zulf, a 23-year old Kashmiri vegetable vendor, would drive this new vehicle. He was cool and positive about our journey.

The team - Sarvesh, Zulf, Dasu, Rath and myself - left for Leh by road from Srinagar in the last week of August. The excitement was at a peak. We met R Anand who flew to Leh from Delhi a day later. After reaching Leh, we acclimatized for a week before the start of the ride. We tested all our bicycles, when it was found that the front wheel of my mountain bicycle needed minimal truing. Several mock rides were carried out in and around Leh.

Srini and R Anand acclimatizing in Leh

At Pathar Sahib Gurudwara in Leh in Aug 2014. L to R: Mariya Dasu, Srini, R Anand, Rathar, Zulf and Sarvesh with the follow van and the bicycles

The day before the ride, Dasu and I tried a hand at fixing the wheel which needed some truing, but we messed it up. We didn't know what to do and there were no bicycle shops open that evening. Three days before the ride, we'd visited Guru, another Air Force officer posted to Leh, and I had spotted a Firefox bicycle at his residence. He most graciously lent us the front wheel on the day of the ride and we were set again.

Finally, on the cold morning of 2nd September 2014, R. Anand and I along with our support crew were finally flagged off from the Leh War Memorial by the Station Commander of Leh Military station and the SBI Branch Manager, Leh.

**Flag-off by Station Commander and SBI branch Manager at 4 am
on 02 Sep 2014 at Leh War memorial**

We started strong at 4:00 A.M as the road slope gradient stayed flat for the first 60 km. The daylight started to trickle in and we spotted a local bicycle shop where we could get my damaged wheel trued. As the roads were good, we were on our road bicycles. However, at a major junction where we were to turn right towards the Tanglang La mountain pass, R. Anand realised he had forgotten his ID (Identity) card. The defence ID card is a very valuable possession for any solider, the loss of which can be penalised by the court. He was sure he was not carrying it with him as he misplaced the bag with the ID card at the War memorial at the time of Flag off early in the morning. I also requested Guru to help us out, as the bag was under the custody of Military Police who spotted it that morning at the War memorial as an unclaimed bag. The support van with the crew had to drive back to Leh while Anand and I waited at an Army establishment along the route. This consumed a lot of time, energy, and focus. It took almost four hours to retrieve the ID card before we could start again.

Anger towards Anand had begun to simmer within me as we had lost a good chunk of time, due to an avoidable error but I held on as we had a long way to go. By afternoon we stopped for lunch at the military camp in Upshi, a small village along the Leh – Manali highway. Once back on our bicycles, the terrain got tougher and the mountains bigger and bigger. I was not performing well; I was breathing hard and had a headache, which I recognised it as symptoms of Acute Mountain Sickness. Each pedal stroke was getting tougher and tougher, tips of my feet numb and I was literally crawling up this mighty pass. The elevation was starting to get to me. Anand was doing good and didn't seem to be suffering.

By the time we reached Tanglang La at 17500 ft at 1930 hr, it was snowing, cold and dark. I dragged myself to the summit, suffering from hypothermia. We then descended down to Pang and reached there by 9:30 P.M.

Climbing Tanglang La pass in bad weather. Pictured: R Anand in the front and Srini behind him

The Military camp at Pang was expecting us earlier that evening. They made place for us to rest and prepared hot food. After a good night's sleep, we were suitably recovered and left for Sarchu by 8:00 A.M. The weather on Day 1 came as a surprise to us. We later found out that there were heavy rains and floods in many parts of Jammu and Kashmir.

The weather forecast was not good for the second day, either. There were mild showers and uphill roads. With high mountains and deserted paths all around, we were cut off from the chaos of the real world. The stretch to Sarchu was around 50 miles/80 km, which seems small, but the two big passes Lachung La and Naki La were a challenge to cross amidst the bad weather.

Srini and R Anand at Lachung La and Nakeela pass

We made it to the Sarchu Base camp by 4:00 P.M. At the camp, a huge German shepherd, the pet of one of the officers, saw me in my cycling attire with the helmet and balaclava, and charged ferociously at me. I was bitten on my left thigh. Fortunately, the flesh was not ripped, but it was painful. I had to take a Tetanus shot and a shot of analgesic.

Early the next morning, we started to Tandi in Himachal Pradesh. The weather was still not great and the flood situation had worsened all over Kashmir with plenty of rain and snowfall.

Sarchu to Tandi is a 80 miles/130 km stretch with one big pass, Barlach La, at a 17000 ft altitude. The inclement weather was making life tough for our team. Nevertheless, we were riding strong and fortunately had found our rhythm, we were doing well.

Srini and R Anand riding towards Barlach La pass.

**Srini and R Anand riding down the Barlach la pass towards Tandi.
Zulf and Dasu busy clicking pictures next to the follow van.**

We reached Tandi before 5:00 P.M. That gave us time to get our bicycles cleaned and the pickup van serviced for our next challenge - crossing the Rohtang pass. At Tandi, Anand was not keeping well. His knees were aching and he was exhausted. I, on the other hand, felt strong and was raring to go but, we needed to sail together.

The next day, the weather was worse at Tandi, crossing Rohtang pass in this weather was a very risky affair. We were warned by many to sit out the day. I insisted that we move on. We were losing time. We would cross Rohtang Pass and hope for the best. With mild rains, and slushy, tortuous roads, it was challenging. It took us considerable time to reach Rohtang Pass.

Zulf was a real professional with amazing driving skills. He put on a grand display on these treacherous routes. This adventure was special to him because he had never been out of Kashmir in his life, I could feel that Zulf was having a good time negotiating tough terrain.

As we reached the top of Rohtang Pass, Anand's knee gave up, earning him a ride down the mountain in the van. I descended like a maniac—a man possessed-- on my mountain bicycle, covering a good distance and making up for lost time. The weather was still bad with thunderstorms and poor visibility, but I rode with intent, taking the downhill slopes head-on until I reached the Pandoh transit camp. It was past midnight, we had been cut off from the real world for the last four days, and were now back to civilization. We discovered that the floods had caused havoc in Kashmir and through the Leh- Manali stretch.

Anand and I decided to take a short sleep break before hopping back on our bicycles by 3:00 A.M. The crew was not adequately rested; fatigue was already acting on each of them. I knew about my crew was exhausted but I failed to address it, even though they felt resting for another few hours. Probably I should have considered it, although we were lagging behind the schedule. The road to Chandigarh was not smooth; we had to cross Swarghat, which is a big, pothole-laden hill that is known for heavy traffic. We lost contact with the support van as the support van sustained a puncture and we riders decided to move ahead on the course while the support van dealt with fixing the puncture. To make matters worse, Anand sustained a flat tyre as we were climbing the hill, we did not have any spares.

We lost around three hours, but rode strong. We reached Chandigarh by 7:00 P.M. and were escorted by military police to a reception that made us feel special. Our day was made.

The expedition team had thus far been in the wilderness and was protected from pollution, traffic and honking. Although faster, Delhi was rough. We reached the India Gate, expecting to be received by a cyclist's group Anand knew, but we were disappointed. It turned out that there had perhaps been a miscommunication. We struggled to find a place to stay the night and finally ended up at Anand's place near the Delhi-Agra highway. The next day we rode the expressway to Agra.

We had weighed the pros and cons before deciding on the Expressway - the path had wide shoulders and a good road surface, but cyclists were not allowed on and we had to seek permission from the highway authorities for our cycles and support van.

Once in Agra, we were given a formal welcome at the military station by the troops in the form of escort by the military police. By this time the team had found great speeds and rhythm. The plan for the following day was to head towards Jhansi in Uttar Pradesh. To keep the ride fair and for purposes of documenting proof, we set a few practices such as taking signatures from gazetted officers at the start and end of every day, collecting ATM withdrawal slips every 100 km, recording photos and videos, and finally saving the GPS data.

Finding a rhythm and going with the flow was the order of the day as we moved south towards Jhansi. The team was sceptical about the road conditions but to our surprise, the road to Jhansi was quite good. We were cruising faster and we reached Jhansi well within time, where we were given an extraordinary reception at the Military station. It was surprising to see the kind of arrangements the station had made for us by the Commanding Officer of one of the Military units which hosted us. He was so excited about this ride and his unit had made all the arrangements in just a few hours. There was a banner put up and the whole station of around 500 troops had gathered to welcome us, not to mention the delicious spread we enjoyed for dinner. We were now upbeat and motivated about this adventure. The next day, we left Jhansi by 3:00 A.M. The unit went the extra mile in arranging for our departure in the wee hours. They arranged Military police to escort us to the highway and they arranged for drinking water, fruits, packed breakfast and lunch for the whole team.

The roads were really good and the route scenic, with small hills along the course. Since the Military Station, Sagar was only at a 100 km distance we did not want to halt there. Instead we rode 350 km and halted at a hotel in Narsinghpur in Madhya Pradesh. This was our first halt at a civil hotel instead of a Military camp.

The Deccan plateau was welcoming the two riders and our crew as we drifted through the rolling terrain and lush green forests of Chindwara. We planned to halt for the night at the Air Force guest rooms in Nagpur, Maharashtra.

We rode from Maharashtra to Andhra Pradesh and were welcomed by roads much worse than the ones witnessed at Rohtang. Here we had to figure out where to stay as Adilabad did not have any Military stations. Sarvesh, our logistics manager, quite impressively got in touch with the NCC (National Cadet Corps) camp at Adilabad and fixed up a place for us to halt.

I felt at home as we rode southwards. Although exhausted, we were on cruise mode and anticipating our next halt at a military station in Hyderabad. We were also in touch with the Hyderabad Cycling Club, who were keen to flag us off along the Bangalore- Hyderabad highway. They were concerned about our team's requirements and also rode with us for around 50 km along the Bangalore- Hyderabad highway. This was the first bicycle club to meet us on our route. We later halted at a hotel in the village of Gooty, around 185 miles/300 km later.

Hyderabad Cycling Club members meeting and greeting the Expedition Team

The stretch from Gooty to Bangalore was relatively easy and reaching Bangalore was a huge accomplishment in itself. The roads were good. We halted at Air Force Station, Yelahanka. I finally had the opportunity to visit my family, borrowing a scooter to ride to Vijayanagar which was 15 miles/25 km away to visit Prafulla and Rohan after almost a month. It was truly worth the effort. I was back in Yelahanka by 11:00 P.M. to rest and ride the next morning. We decided to get back on the road by 4:00 A.M.

No one else in the team was ready at that time. I lost my temper with the support crew and Anand, who in turn got irritated with my outburst. It took us a while but eventually, everyone cooled down and got on with the task ahead of us. We rode strong till Salem, where we halted for four hours and decided we would ride all through the night to Madurai. Again, we managed to find an NCC camp to halt for a couple of hours, and by 7:00 P.M., we were pedalling towards Madurai.

This was the last night of our journey. We kept riding until we reached Madurai by early morning, and kept rolling towards Kanyakumari. On our way there, we cycled through the second largest wind zone of Asia with thousands of windmills along the stretch. The headwinds were so strong, they nearly threw us off our bicycles. Finally, around 10:00 P.M. we made it to Kanyakumari, the southernmost tip of India. The final point of our ride was at Vivekananda's Rock, where we clicked pictures and got the ride attested at the Police Station. Anand's mother surprised the team by landing up at Kanyakumari to greet us.

The Expedition team at Vivekananda rock, Kanyakumari in Sep 2014.

The data was assimilated; the expedition had been completed in 15 days and 22 hours. The log book was duly filled and signed by necessary authorities, and all the relevant data was submitted to the Limca Book of Records. We had beaten the previous record by 3 days.

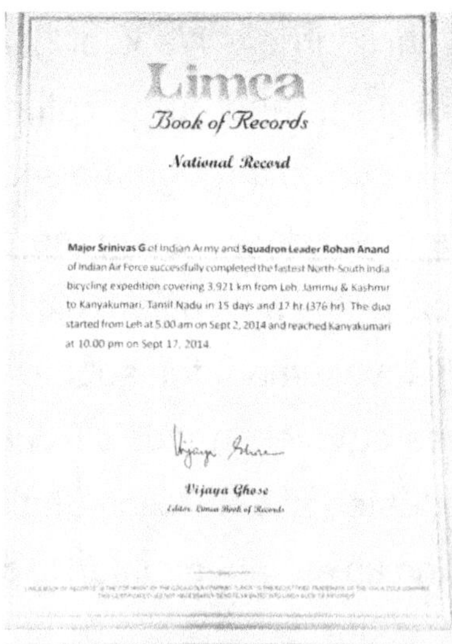

The Certificate from Limca Book of Records and Srini and R Anand at Kanyakumari

An amazing ride by my team and I had come to an end. I had dreamt about it, worked towards it and with the help of my crew, achieved it!

Anand flew back to Delhi, while my team and I drove northwards to Kashmir. I got off at Bangalore and Dasu in Hyderabad. The brave Sarvesh, Zulf and Rath drove all the way back to Srinagar, which had been badly affected by the floods.

5. LICENCE TO DREAM

Since 2009, I had aspired to participate in and successfully complete Race Across America (RAAM). Now, having checked off the precursory goal of the Leh-Kanyakumari ride, I felt like I was almost there. I had been called to complete four weeks of administrative training in Lucknow and eight weeks of professional training in Pune with the Military starting in October 2014. In the last week of October, I came across a Facebook post by Divya Tate regarding the RAAM Qualifying Race being held in Pune on 29 November 2014. Divya Tate was the race director of the Deccan Cliffhanger Race, a RAAM qualifier held each year from Pune to Goa. I was in Lucknow, and this post got me all fired up, even though I was busy with my course and moreover had neither a bicycle nor a support team. For the second phase of the course, I landed in Pune in the last week of October 2014. The registrations for the event were scheduled for the last week of November. I made up my mind to give it a try.

With my mind set on this goal, I found a way to borrow a bicycle from a cycling friend Sumit Dwivedi in Bangalore, and also went ahead with using Prafulla's Nano car as my support vehicle. So, the training began. I would ride to Singhad fort and Lavassa at 4:00 A.M. I was also setting up my crew; a mandatory two person who were required to know how to drive and hold a valid driving licence.

There were two mandatory Military Medicine exams scheduled for 29th November 2014, which was clashing with the race day. At that stage things looked bleak but I still wanted to try. I requested my instructor to postpone the test by another day. It was a rare possibility, but I was lucky enough to get the permission. Now that the major hurdle had been crossed, I tried sifting through my connections to find myself a crew. I was put in touch with the Cymour Bicycling Group and went on a weekend ride with them immediately. This was where I met Arham and Aniket. Arham Sheikh was a young college student, a Defence aspirant and also an amateur rower. He and Aniket Mhasavade, the creator of the Cymour group, were both incredibly excited by my cycling adventures and agreed to be a part of Team Srini. It always felt great interacting with and finding support within the cycling community.

Arham was very resourceful in finding more support as his college friends, Sid and Utsav, also volunteered to join our team. We all met up for a team briefing and the plan was chalked out. Following this, regular team meetings were held and it was decided that Aniket would be the team director, Sid would take care of food and hydration, Utsav would be our primary driver and Arham the Race Marshal. Aniket was kind enough to offer me a new Merida road bicycle and other accessories for the race. With this terrific crew backing me, I was all set to give 100%. On the day before the race, our support car, a black minivan (Innova) with a PA system was set. We were ready to go!

D DAY

There was festivity in the air as riders, with their support crew and the media, flocked to the starting point of the race. Our team was called Cymour Spirits. I rode strong. In the next couple of hours, we were in the second position behind a rider named Apurv. At the descent of Mahabaleshwar, I overtook him and was in the first position for a long time-- till 2:00 P.M. At that point, I was 120 km away from Kolhapur. Exhaustion was setting in Apurv and three other racers blazed past me. I had not been consuming enough food and fluids (a minimum of 200 calories and 500 ml of fluids with electrolytes is essential to enduring such a race). Aniket worked out a solution. He said, "Take a short 10-

minute break every hour for the next four hours from 6 pm and just eat whatever we give you." I had to agree and started following the team's instructions. I reached Kittur by 3:30 A.M. and did not want to sleep, but the team forced me to nap for 15 minutes. By 4:00 A.M. I was working out the math in my head and realized that I would have to go all out, all the way till the end. I rode hard, reaching Belgaum by 6:00 A.M. I did not stop. I continued to Chorla Ghat, a particularly tricky point as it is a hill with no summit and you just keep going round and round the hill. As I approached the last checkpoint, the team was excited about a successful finish. At that moment, Aniket received a call from Divya, informing us that the cut off time was 1:15 P.M. We were two hours short of it. Many doubts were running in my mind, but that is when my belief came in handy. My crew was constantly motivating me, "Srini! You have ridden across the country a distance of 2500 miles and riding 400 miles is a piece of cake". I started believing myself more and more. The last 40 km stretch was a difficult rolling terrain that the two leading racers had taken two and half hours to complete. I refused to give up and rode at a 25 mile/40 km average pace, knowing I'd get there, but still wanting to push hard. My team was constantly motivating me. In fact, we encountered an 800 metre stretch of a traffic jam, just 12 mile/20 km short of the finish line at Bogmola beach. That's when Aniket shouted out to carry on and to take a left turn at the intersection. I continued as advised. The stats for the last stretch was 10 kms to be completed in one hour, and the rolling terrain continued. I was looking out for the finish line when I spotted the Deccan Cliffhanger banners to the left of the road. I had made it well in time with 45 minutes to spare. Relieved and ecstatic about the team's efforts, we found that I had finished third in the race. I was very happy and was deeply thankful to my crew. I had qualified for the Race Across America!

From Pune, I returned to Srinagar in December 2014. I got an opportunity to meet the Generals who had felicitated me for the Limca Record. Prafulla and Rohan joined me there in February 2015. I had made up my mind to prepare for RAAM, but was under the impression that being in Srinagar, I would not be able to prepare due to security concerns with moving out of the garrison. I was vehemently trying to get out of Srinagar and get posted to Pune.

In July 2015, I moved out of Srinagar to my new place of work in Nashik, Maharashtra and was filled with uncertainty and apprehension about whether this place would be favourable to pursue my RAAM ambitions.

The Deccan Cliffhanger (TDC) 3, 07-08 NOV 15

The Temple City of Nashik in Maharashtra, known for its vineyards, was our next destination and the setting to my exploration of the possibilities to attempt RAAM in 2016. I had exactly one year. But the nature of my work at this new place was a very engaging and strenuous. I still sought the silver lining and tried to create the space to pursue my training. In June 2015, there was a two-man team, the Mahajan Brothers (Hitendra Mahajan and Mahendra Mahajan) from Nashik, who had finished RAAM in the team category. That was an upside to me being in Nashik, so I tried to learn more about the race through them. They helped me understand the American continent from the racer's perspective. Mahendra Mahajan was also willing to share information on the terrain, weather, and various logistical challenges involved in the race. This helped me prepare mentally. Attending many of their felicitation ceremonies, I was motivated by the kind of support and admiration they got from the people in Nashik. Meanwhile, I was also exploring routes in and around Nashik that were conducive to cycling.

It was in the month of September 2015 that I learnt just how phenomenal the expenditure for RAAM would be. Factoring in the registration fees, air tickets, accommodation, and support vehicles, and then considering that the US dollar is 70 times stronger than the Indian rupee, I realised I would undoubtedly need sponsorship. I also knew I'd need a bicycle upgrade and many other accessories and logistics to participate. By September 2014, I invested in a new bicycle; the Neilpryde BURA SL which was quite expensive, from a bicycle Shop in Mumbai. It was a big cut in the meagre resources that I had. I was also doing a lot of Randoneeuring rides in Nashik. Randoneeuring, also known as Audax, is a long-distance cycling sport where riders attempt courses of 200 km or more, passing through predetermined "controls" (checkpoints) every few tens of kilometres. Riders aim to complete the course within specified time limits and receive equal recognition regardless of their finishing order. Riders may travel in groups or alone as they wish, and are expected to be self-sufficient between controls. In the same month I came to know about the race, The Deccan Cliffhanger (TDC) 3rd edition, which I did in 2014.

I wanted to test out my new bicycle and also gather and train my crew for RAAM. I was making use of the race to train for RAAM. Being in need of a crew, I approached the Nasik Cyclists Group for support, but was not lucky enough to find a prompt response and I went ahead with my own jugaad. I sought help from my previous crew in Pune, but found that Arham was participating in the race as a rider. He did, however, put me in touch with a few other potential candidates, out of whom Dhruv Shah, a young amateur cyclist from Pune, was chosen. He was keen on becoming a professional cyclist and had been regularly training to make it to the state-level competitions. Dhruv's mother was one of the race officials of The Deccan Cliffhanger race. Niranjan Upasani was the other crew member whom I had met in 2014 while meeting potential sponsors in Pune. He was a businessman and I found him to be capable of crewing. I also managed to get two of my workplace buddies, Dhanasekar (Dhana) and Sukhdev Singh on board and trained them on bicycle mechanics, navigation, and nutrition.

Dhana was a professional Physiotherapist and was good at his job. He worked with patients with neurological deficits, spastic children, and also with injured sportsmen.

Sukhdev was a radio technician and had a unique ability to fix things, with his engineering-inclined brain.

I formed my crew with Niranjan as Crew Chief, Dhana as Physiotherapist, and Sukhdev as the driver. We charted out a strategy for this race. Our level of preparedness was improving as race day neared. My Neilpryde Bura SL was the primary bicycle and the Giant TCR 3 the secondary bicycle. Although I knew it was a tough race for me and that our preparation was perhaps not sufficient in all spheres, especially training and nutrition, I still rode 600 km before the race on the new bicycle. The whole race was discussed in totality on a WhatsApp Group named 'Team Srini'. I firmly believed that the support crew should be well-educated about the race format, its challenges, and so on and thereby be well prepared for any eventuality.

On 5 November 2015, the bicycles and support car were set for the race inspection. Our dedicated team, full of good energy, left for Pune via Mumbai. It took us five hours to reach Deccan Gymkhana, Pune. There we met Niranjan and Dhruv for the first time and also met Divya Tate and Fred Boethling, Race Director for RAAM. The crew and I were extremely excited.

The next morning, we gathered all our necessities for race day from a supermarket and then headed to the registration desk at Café Nook. Here, we surprised the race officials with our preparation, and we were done with all the pre-race registration formalities in one go, thanks to Sukhdev who had worked out our logistics so well in advance.

RACE DAY

The night before the race, I was unable to stop worrying and working out one contingency plan after the other. It was not easy to let go of these unwanted thoughts, and it led to disturbed sleep that night. The entire team was up by 2:45 A.M. As always, there was awesome energy at the starting point; lots of zeal and positivity emanated from all the riders and crews.

We were off to a decent start, but getting out of the Pune suburbs was a challenge in itself. I lost contact with my crew before the Katraj tunnel and was in desperate need of water. Sumit Patil, another solo racer was riding along and sensed my need, and quite kindly offered me a bottle of water. My crew was having problems with the support car, hence the delay in catching up with following me.

The next uphill was the traffic-infested Khambatki, but I managed to ride safe. I was still completely separated from my crew, but finally met up with them at the toll booth.

I pushed hard through the Panchagani and Mahabaleswar climb, and saw a decent descent, except for one turn where I misjudged a curve completely, and nearly collided head-on with an approaching car on the opposite side of the road. I managed to move to the extreme right end of the road just in time. By Check Point #1, I was riding strong and fast with an overall standing at second place, just a few minutes behind the race leader.

I kept riding strong. Eventually, I decided to have a proper meal and sat down somewhere along the highway, but could not eat any solid food. I drank buttermilk instead. That was when I saw a couple of riders passing by. After some stretching, I got back on the saddle, but 40 minutes into the ride I felt really nauseated and had multiple bouts of vomiting. I stopped riding. While I was going through this agony, I witnessed a horrific crash. The race officials' car had been hit by a state transport bus. I watched the car fly into a ditch with alarm! Miraculously, all were safe. Amazing work was done by Niranjan and other crew members of my team, as they rescued a couple of them. In the meantime, Dhruv was pushing me to get back on the bicycle and start riding. I started again but was not feeling good, still nauseated and avoiding any oral intake. In no time I was overtaken by many solo riders. Finally, I stopped the race and told my crew, "I am not going to ride and want to abandon the race." The crew were shocked.

They did not want to give up on me. After all, they had been taking care of me like a mother does her child - feeding me, cleaning me, changing my clothes, giving me a massage, putting me to sleep. They said, "You just ride, we are with you."

I had lost a couple of hours by then, but I resolved to get back on the saddle and revive my position in the race. The crew made me fresh tomato juice, apple juice and orange juice. I was still struggling to find a rhythm, frequently getting off the saddle for no apparent reason. We reached Kolhapur at the 13th Hour and were doing fairly well, when I met Rahul Kotabage, another solo rider. It was nice to ride with him and his crew, so we decided to stick around with them.

Team Srini came back stronger in the second half of the race and we were making good ground to finish within 32 hours. Then came the hilly section of the mystique Chorla via Amboli. I cautioned my crew to be very vigilant with the navigation and told them the real fight began now. The support crew lost their way and a good amount of time was lost once again. I was frustrated but controlled myself this time and restored faith in my crew.

I survived, and finished within 30 hours and 35 min. Incidentally, it was also 8 November, my birthday! I had qualified for RAAM again. I tried to connect with the winner of the race, Michael Lehnig, a German living in India who had finished ten hours ahead of me. I was keen on learning how to improve my racing abilities, and Michael agreed to talk about my future plans later that month.

Srini at the finish line of The Deccan Cliffhanger race in 2014 and 2015, L to R: Utsav, Aniket, Sid, Srini, Arham, Srini again, Sukhdev

I and Michael Lehnig met in the third week of November 2015 in Pune. Michael Lehnig was a German citizen in Pune who was working as a fitness and a Cycling coach. He was a 35-year-old young strong athlete, a hard task master, no non sense kind of a guy. He was serious about cycling and had high expectations of himself. I was very impressed with the way he won the Deccan Cliffhanger race in 2015 in a record time. I felt there is so much to learn from him. On my first meeting in Pune after the race he was very understanding and we discussed about what are our expectations from each other. We worked out the timelines, training structure and the training fees. He sounded very professional and promising.

During this visit to Pune, I had also planned to meet an eminent Sports Medicine specialist Dr Cruz at his sports lab (Krumur sports lab) for objective assessment of my fitness level. At the Krumur Sports Lab, Dr.Cruz conducted an array of tests and Michael was also around to check on my performance. The doctor ran several biochemical and fitness tests to ascertain where I stood in terms of basic and specific cycling fitness. Specific tests such as VO2 Max, Lactate threshold heart rate, Bicycle ergometry, body fat analysis, core strength, and flexibility assessment were carried out. I was way below the average athlete as per the test results. Dr Cruz bluntly told me I was not ready for RAAM and advised me to prepare for another year before participating. I was emotional with this dilemma - whether to do RAAM in 2016 or postpone it to 2017. I knew that no Indian had ever finished this race and I had a gut feeling that I might miss that title if I waited until 2017. I expressed this to Michael and said I would give my absolute best towards the training that he suggested for the next 6 months. I was unwilling to even consider postponing it to 2017. Michael agreed to train me in the next 6 months for RAAM 2016. I was excited.

6. IGNORANCE DIARIES

I was diligently following the training schedule that Michael had chalked up for December 2015. I was working towards building a support crew, registering for the race, finding sponsors, and trying to best understand RAAM. Life was busy even apart from my routine Senior Medical Officer job at the medical wing of The Artillery Centre in Nashik. The training plan for December focused on short low-volume and low-intensity rides, and was aimed at setting up the stage for subsequent high-volume rides. Michael was closely monitoring my progress.

It was January 2016. I continued to train according to the plan but now the volume of rides was increasing significantly. Michael wanted me to ride 250 km for three consecutive days and then a 300 km ride on the weekend. It was challenging. I had a tough time logging the required volume of rides as the three consecutive rides had to be carried out on weekdays, amidst my day job at the medical centre. I would try to log 60 miles/100 km in the morning and 95 miles/150 km in the evening. It was not easy and Michael was not very happy when I skipped my training on few days. In fact, he clearly expressed his doubts over my participation in RAAM, as I had been unable to meet the training demands. Michael kept telling me that I was underperforming and that I was not strong enough, and also expressed his concern about coaching. "If you still intend for me to train you, you've got to be consistent and stick to the training schedule. Else it is a waste of time and money for us both." I promised Michael I would stick to the plan.

The next month, I registered for the race and my name appeared on the RAAM website. I had approached many people who had crewed for the Mahajan Brothers in Nashik. Two of them, Mohinder and Milind, agreed to crew for me but I would have to sponsor their travel and accommodation. I had also launched a crowdfunding campaign, which my medical school friend, Kokila Krishnamurthy, helped in running and also pitched in for. Most of my Medical school friends were forthcoming; I had also requested my school friend Kishore Gopalakrishna, who lived in California, to help with rental vans and accommodations. The other crew members---Dhanashekar, Sukhdev Singh, and Niranjan Upasani--were supposed to work on passports and our visas. All that while, I continued to train, build my crew, and work on logistics. With respect to training, Michael was still not happy and continued to rebuke and intimidate me, but also invited me to go to Pune and train with him for a week.

In March, Kishore reassured me about accommodation and rental vans in the US. I went to Pune to train with Michael and to meet the probable sponsors, while the other crew members worked on our visas. Michael rode with me every day during the seven-day training plan - we rode 300 km every day for three consecutive days, took a break, and repeated this for the next three days. Michael was way stronger than I was in these training rides. After 7 days of training, there was a debriefing scheduled by Michael at his place where my crew member, Niranjan, and a potential sponsor were also present. Michael during debriefing said, "Srini is not prepared for RAAM 2016, it would be a waste of time and resources to spend on him". Needless to say, I felt bad with Michael being so harsh on me. I returned to Nasik with some good training, but bad spirits. Along with Dhana and Sukhdev, I focused on procuring the US visas, which I got but Dhana and Sukhdev were denied. Out of the five shortlisted crew members, only two had their US visas. Stress was piling on me; I was overwhelmed by everything around me.

On 1 April 2016, I got a call from Michael, who said, "I am not finding it worthwhile to coach you; you don't seem to understand commitment. I would love to be part of a winning team in RAAM, but not a losing team like yours. I'd prefer to back out from coaching and crewing with you". I was shattered. I always felt Michael did not completely believe in me, he was certain that I was not capable enough to do RAAM and that was conveyed in many ways by him during the training. When I was not able to finish the prescribed training, he used to vent out this feeling that I am not fit enough. This made me more defensive and less motivated, I started to believe that yes, I may not be strong enough. This vicious cycle went on and on and consumed both of us I guess and that made him to quit. Michael had been sharing monthly training plans with me and I would report back to him on a weekly basis. I hadn't been doing too well in terms of clocking the monthly mileage he had set for me. Yet, Michael backing out came as a shock. I spoke to Prafulla about this and she, too, was quite upset. I now had only three crew members out of which two were willing to join only if their travel is sponsored. Niranjan had his US visa and was ready to self-sponsor his travel. Dhana and Sukhdev applied for their visas another couple of times, but were still denied. The other two crew members from Nashik gave up on me, too. Other than Niranjan, I had no crew. All this while, Prafulla had been silently observing everything going on with this venture. She had watched me struggling and did her best to support me even though I hadn't been able to show up as the companion she needed, due to my preoccupation with RAAM. Looking at me in this helpless situation, my dear wife volunteered to crew for me out of nowhere. She wanted me to work on obtaining a visa for her travel and thankfully both Prafulla and Rohan got their visas. She was all set to crew! Prafulla encouraged me to focus on my training and not to dilute those efforts. She truly turned out to be my strongest supporter. Dhana tried for his visa for the fourth time and finally succeeded in getting it. I was very happy with these developments. Now I had three crew members with their US visas in hand. Kishore in the US agreed to crew for Team Srini, as well. Now we were four. I approached some of my cycling acquaintances in Bangalore and amongst them, found help in Gyani, Venky, and Shreyas. They all applied for their visas and were successful. Finally, I had a crew, with Niranjan as Crew Chief, Dhana as the physiotherapist, Prafulla as the Medic and Nutritionist, Gyani as a navigator, Venky as the bicycle mechanic, and Shreyas and Kishore as drivers.

I preferred to do altitude training in Ooty, Tamil Nadu. Prafulla also wanted to join me there along with Rohan. I had thought of doing it alone, but agreed to make it a training-come-family-trip for Rohan, since we had decided to leave him back in India with his grandparents while we participated in RAAM. I trained for five days in Ooty and logged 500 km. Prafulla, Rohan, and I returned to Nashik. Rohan was 2-½ years old and was still being breastfed by Prafulla.

I managed to raise some finances through the crowdfunding campaign. One of the sponsors agreed to help with the air tickets for me and my crew. I was finally relieved. The air tickets were booked for the whole team. Dhana, Niranjan and I were travelling on 27 May 2016 to San Francisco and the rest leaving for Los Angeles on 7 June 2016. Kishore backed off from crewing, citing his busy work schedule, but by now I was used to people dropping off from the team.

On 28 May 2016, we landed in San Francisco, where I met Kishore after a long gap of 24 years. He hosted us at his home, making space for us and also working to get us the required logistics. He also helped me get acclimated to training on US roads. He really did his best to help

Team Srini prepare for the race. A hip-hop themed campervan painted in dashing colours had been booked by Kishore as one of our support vehicles. It managed to catch all eyes on the road and we left for Anaheim after staying at Kishore's place for five days.

The camper van, as one of the follow vehicles for RAAM 2016.
Temecula, California

Prafulla and the rest of the team landed in Los Angeles by 07 June and all six crew members stayed in one room in Anaheim that day. The next day, we planned to pick up another follow van, but had issues with payment options. Once again, Kishore was helpful and could sort out the vehicle issue from San Francisco. We drove down to Temecula as Kishore had booked us an Airbnb for a week. The hosts at Temecula were Adam Morris and his sweet family, hosting Indians for the first time. Team Srini were seven in number and we squeezed ourselves into two different rooms in the house. We used a common kitchen and Adam and his family enjoyed the Indian food we prepared. Prafulla did her best to gel with the crew and ensured that we were all well fed before the race. On 10 Jun 2016 we also celebrated our fourth marriage anniversary along with the crew at Temecula, California.

I received an unexpected phone call from Kishore, who told me he was willing to crew for us. I was very happy to have him back on board.

Srini and Kishore Gopalakrishna, an evening before the start of the RAAM 2016 at Oceanside Pier

The preparations to set up the follow-vehicle and to ride the first 60 miles of the race course was undertaken. Everything was going well. All seemed new for most of the team members and it took us a while to actually understand the vastness of the USA. The last three days before the race were spent on race formalities and further developing the strategy. We all attended the pre-race inspections and crew chiefs' meeting. There are 55-time stations along the race route. Each time station needs to be reported as a rider crossed it. There is a GPS tracker with each rider that tracked us all throughout the 12 days. Kishore joined the team two days before the race, and stayed with me, constantly motivating me to give my best and to not give up. I was excited and waiting to start off on 14 Jun 2016. The night before the race, we finalized the strategy and came to terms with the challenges that we were about to face.

Srini and part of his crew at Pacific Coast, Oceanside Pier, L to R: Srini, Prafulla, Niranjan, Dhana, Shreyas.

On 14 June 2016, the start line of the race at the pier in Oceanside, California along the West coast of Pacific Ocean was buzzing with cyclists around the world. We were all on the edge of taking on the race of our lives. The excited cyclists with their crew and crew vans lent to the merriness and exhilaration of the proceedings at the pier. And there I was, blissfully unaware of the beast of a race that I was about to undertake. At 1:10 P.M.—at long last-- I was flagged off, My Race Across America had begun! After almost seven years of dreaming, I was here. Now the 3000 miles/5000 km to be pedalled lay ahead of me. The race started with riders cycling along the unsupported race route for about 23 miles and subsequently we get in touch with our respective support crew.

Srini at the starting line of RAAM 2016 at Oceanside, California

Two hours into the race, Srini climbing towards Time Station 1, Lake Henshaw. His crew member Dhana is behind him. Another solo racer in Pink is also seen in the picture

From there onward, I was overtaken by many solo riders. They blazed past me at Lake Henshaw (Time station 1). I felt, I was riding too slow. I needed to conserve energy for the days to come. I reached the summit of the Glass Elevator and descended carefully into the plains. The Glass elevator is the road that descends quickly into Borrego Springs from Lake Henshaw. It is San Diego County's sustained grade road. The Glass elevator name describes the rapid descent and ever widening desert views as if one is seeing everything while riding in a glass elevator. The sweeping desert floor views of Borrego Springs are breath taking.

At Christmas Circle of Borrego Springs, I met the other crew members Niranjan, Prafulla, and Venky, but kept moving on without stopping. We reached Brawley at 11.P.M local time. The crew sensed that I was riding very slow but they didn't force me that night, and I rode all night.

A lot happened with the crew in that camper van - there were communication issues that started to erupt between Niranjan, Prafulla, and Venky. Prafulla was keen to know why I was not riding stronger and faster. I reached Time Station 3 in Blythe, California, early morning on 15 June and then rode to Time Station 4 in Parker, Arizona in the next six hours. From there, I went on to Time Station 5 in Salome, Arizona. I was battling extreme heat in the deserts of Arizona.

I was dangerously slow on the bicycle and the crew was already losing hope. Plenty of negative thoughts were flowing in both the vans. Niranjan in the camper van remarked that I was not prepared and was wasting time. Prafulla was offended and told him not to give up and to fight till the end. Prafulla communicated with Kishore, who was handling the entire operations by this point and by default he became the crew chief of Team Srini now. Kishore told me to pick up some speed. I reached Time Station 6 in Congress, Arizona that night.

Srini riding through the deserts of Arizona with his crew member Gyani trying to cool him down with a sprayer. The day time temperatures soaring at 50° Celsius or 105° Fahrenheit

On 16th June, I climbed two big uphill slopes to reach Time Station 7 in Prescott, Arizona in the morning and then dragged myself to Time Station 8 in Camp Verde, Arizona by afternoon. Onward from there was that 100 mile/160 km long stretch to Time Station 9 in Flagstaff, Arizona, it took a long time. I was feeling sleepy and cold in the night. Niranjan, still in the camper van, kept commenting that there was no point in me continuing the race. It would be better to abandon and go on a road trip instead. Prafulla and Venky were frustrated with Niranjan's attitude and snapped at him to just drive the camper van and to not worry about me. Kishore and Shreyas kept pushing me, even though I was struggling to stay on the saddle.

Desert with arid vegetation on the route between Salome, Arizona and Congress, Arizona

I somehow dragged myself to Flagstaff by 8:00 A.M. am on June 17. By this point, I had given up on the race, too. I felt I would not be able to make it to the cut off at Durango with the current average speed. I kept telling myself that I had not trained well enough for this task and eventually succumbed to the mental calculations, telling me that I wouldn't make it to Durango in 81 hours.

The Time Station in Durango, Colorado (Time Station 15) was a kind of a staging point. Racers who reach here later than 81 hours into the race aren't allowed to move forward. I expressed my concerns to the crew who then put me to sleep for 1-½ hours. When I woke up, I said I was done; that I was giving up. Prafulla and Kishore told me to get on the bicycle and ride to the next time station in Tuba City, Arizona (Time Station 10). I rode there quite poorly. A zombie ride. By Tuba City, the whole crew had given up on me, except Prafulla and Venky.

Team Srini was hanging around at McDonalds and lazed there for three hours. At around 3:30 P.M. local time, I decided to ride till the next time station. I was hesitant. I had given up on the RAAM dream by this point. I had lost focus on the race. But Venky pushed me to reach Kayenta, Arizona (Time Station 11) by 10:10 P.M. local time. I rode strong and was enjoying the ride thoroughly till we reached Kayenta. Until this stage, no one on the crew knew that Time Station 15 in Durango was a soft cut-off. This meant that a racer could continue with the race even though he had not made it there within the cut-off time.

Team Srini was riding only to make it to Kayenta. Once in Kayenta, I was feeling so strong that I asked my crew for permission to ride further. That's when we realized that it was a soft cut-off and we were all happy to know that we were still alive in the race.

After a shower break, Team Srini left Kayenta with a lot of energy.

The next time stations, Mexican Hat, Utah (Time Station 12) and Montezuma Creek, Utah (Time Station 13) had me performing quite well, but later my motivation started dropping again. I was sleep deprived and exhausted.

Sunrise at Mexican Hat, Utah

Srini riding towards Montezuma Creek

It was 18th June. The journey to Time Station 14 in Cortez, Colorado was one hell of a ride. I was struggling to breathe. It felt like a hypersensitive reaction in my airways to the pollen around. I hid this from my crew for a while. But as I neared Cortez, I started wheezing, my whole respiratory tract was choked with phlegm. I was coughing up blood-specked sputum.

As I made my way to Cortez, I spotted a big guy running along with me and telling me not to give up. He was cheering me on and motivating me to believe and keep pedalling. He managed to chat with Kishore in the follow-van, asking him to take care of the rider. This guy ran with me for almost a kilometre, and it was found that he was Alberto Blanco, a RAAM solo finisher who was crewing for a rider participating in the Race Across the West (RAW).

I reached Cortez, took a sleep break, started on antibiotics for that stretch, and was back on the bicycle. I reached Durango in the evening and stopped for an hour. Kishore, who was excited about the team making it to Durango, surprised me with a big cake. We all got back to work as 40 Time stations / 2100 miles (3400 km) were yet to be covered.

Srini reaches Durango the first cut-off point in the race, although way past the cut-off time, the crew are happy to celebrate the

moments of making it to Durango. L to R: Kishore, Srini, Shreyas, Venky, Gyani, Dhana, Niranjan and Prafulla

The next day, I was on my way to the high Rocky Mountains of Colorado, and was all charged up for Wolf Creek Pass. At this juncture, my bicycle chain snapped. I was forced to change my bicycle to one I had never used before, but I was fortunate enough to scale Wolf Creek with decent timing. The descent from there onward was a struggle.

At the summit of Wolf Creek Pass with the Indian flag. L to R: Venky, Gyani, Niranjan, Shreyas, Srini, Prafulla, Dhana and Kishore

We reached South Fork, Colorado (Time Station 17) and took an hour break and was given an ultimatum to ride faster by my crew. The Ultimatum was that Kishore would leave in between and the crew will pack up midway if I did not ride strong. I did manage to ride stronger, covering three Time Stations - Alamosa, La Veta, and finally Trinidad, all in Colorado.

On 20th June, we reached Trinidad, Colorado (Time Station 20) and slept there for an hour before riding into Walsh, Colorado (Time Station 22, the last time station in Colorado). When we crossed Colorado into Kansas, the crosswinds there were demoralizing me. Though having favourable flat terrains, when the wind blows in Kansas it takes everything with it. I was already exhausted by the time we reached Ulysses, Kansas (Time Station 23). The hot head winds and crosswinds only made it tougher; like someone had turned up a blower right onto your face at full speed. I stopped and got off my bicycle multiple times. I was zombie riding once again.

I struggled the next day but covered two-time stations. On 22nd June, I rode stronger to El Dorado, Kansas (Time Station 28), took a shower at the YMCA camp, and made it to Yates Center (Time Station 29) by the night.

The next time station at Fort Scott, Kansas (Time Station 30) was 80 km away and I was drained. It was pitch dark and I experienced severe visual and auditory hallucinations for six hours. I felt like I was riding in circles inside a shopping mall and the large electric poles in the farms looked like giant moving robots to me. I saw people lying in sleeping bags on the pavements and felt like somebody was holding me up and not letting me move forward. I expressed all such hallucinations to my crew, who were shocked to see me in this condition. They continued to push me for almost six hours and then I could finally sleep once we got to Fort Scott.

By 24th June, we moved out of the state of Kansas and entered Missouri. The rolling terrain helped me ride stronger and at this stage, I had run out of the time given to reach Mississippi. The crew requested the race officials to keep us alive in the race. I was once again excited to be back on the bicycle, made it to Jefferson City (Time Station 33), slept for a while there and then headed to Washington, Missouri (Time Station 34). After this I was fighting my way out to the Mississippi River (Time Station 35) with quite boring and monotonous landscapes.

At the Mississippi the next day, I felt like a hero for getting that far. We rested for an hour and I was back on my bicycle, making my way to Bloomington, Indiana. It was here at Time Station 39, that I met Dave Tanner, who was a volunteer at the Time Station. Dave Tanner, a 60-year-old tall, fit gentleman, who was himself a RAAM finisher and an Olympic swimming coach. When I met him for the first time, Dave encouraged me not to give up and told me to stay on the saddle; that I just might make it to the finish line. He felt for me, as I was fighting a lost battle, and Dave's concern helped me find a friend who would have a strong impact on me and my life. When I left that Time Station, Dave ran with me for about 50 m and insisted not to give up.

After that emotionally charged moment, I dragged myself to Time Station 40 in Greensburg, Indiana, where Kishore declared that he was abandoning the crew and going back home to California. He had been motivating me to ride stronger but had now reached his threshold of exhaustion, and had lost hope on me. He was done and wanted to quit. Although I was at a loss for words, I thanked Kishore for all that he had done for me; it was an emotional moment for us both. I lost one of my strongest crew members at Greensburg.

I kept moving ahead to Time Station 41 in Oxford, Ohio, but with a heavy heart and a worried mind. I was around 460 miles/750 km away from the finish line and had only 27 hours in hand. The mental calculations began and I was left questioning whether I could realistically make it on time or not. The calculations told me I could not, and I fell prey to the workings of my own mind and considered dropping out once I reached Time Station 41.

At TS 41 I said to my crew, "I'm done." Their responses varied. Venky and Shreyas said, "it's the best thing to do." Dhana and Gyani were silent, Niranjan was the least bothered. Prafulla was upset about this decision. She insisted I should keep going as we had another 27 hours, and she thought it was worth trying to continue as far as possible in the race.

At this time station, I met a lady named Lisa Brunckhorst, who was a time station volunteer. She was extremely positive, cheerful and very caring. She, too, was a RAAM race veteran and offered the team cookies, pastries, juices and sandwiches. Lisa understood the situation in terms of me wanting to quit. Prafulla, on the other hand, was surprised and angry that no crew member was in favour of pushing their rider till the last minute. Prafulla said she would be extremely unhappy if I quit the race, while I tried to justify that continuing in the race would not help anyone. Prafulla finally gave up on me, but she said, "Let's at least drive down to the finish line and see how the finishers relish success. Let's see what it means or what it takes to get there." Lisa seconded Prafulla's idea. After some deliberation, the team and I agreed to drive down to the finish line at Annapolis, Maryland. I hopped into the campervan and we began our journey to the East coast. I took a nap during the journey and the crew stopped at a motel to take a shower and rest. We finally reached the place where the banquet ceremony was being held for successful finishers at Annapolis.

The famous bridge on the race route while entering the state of West Virginia. On our way to the East Coast in the support van

The crew and I were exhausted but confident as we walked toward the banquet hall. I was all beaten up; sun burnt and was looking horrible. At the entrance of the hall, we saw Fred Boethling, the Race Director of RAAM. Fred took one look at me and asked, "Did you get a taste of RAAM?" That question churned a lot of emotions in my already battered and bruised mind. I felt bad and did not know how to answer. I was numb. At that moment, Prafulla responded to Fred saying, "He is going to come back next year and he is going to be the first Indian to finish RAAM". I was surprised and shocked to hear Prafulla's spontaneity of response. That was the moment I fully understood how much Prafulla desired to see me succeed at RAAM. In a few minutes, Prafulla and I decide to register for the race next year at the earliest.

Team Srini went on with the evening looking awestruck at the finishers. I congratulated many racers who had finished successfully. One of them was Chris O Keefe from California, USA. When I congratulated him, Chris responded with a question, "What happened to your race?" I told him I had cycled till Time Station 41, but could not continue further. Chris said he understood the pain, as he also had not finished in his first attempt in 2014. Chris and I had a short but strong, moving conversation in that brief interaction.

The crew and I drove up to New York and stayed at Venky's friend's place for a day. The next day, we boarded our flights back to India.

I had cycled 2460 miles in 11 days.

7. FINDING A TALISMAN

28 Jun 2016, Mumbai

Prafulla, Dhana, and I landed in Mumbai and drove down to Nashik in a minivan by midnight. I remember gazing at the Nashik- Mumbai highway where I had trained for RAAM 2016, and now I was thinking about how I would have to redo the entire process for the next year. As we reached home early in the morning, the only thing we were excited about was seeing Rohan, whom we had both missed for more than a month. It was tough even on my son, who had been breast fed till about a month ago, and had to let go of that when Prafulla left for RAAM.

We were back to our routine jobs by 1 July 2016. Prafulla and I started analysing the race retrospectively - what went right, what went wrong, and what needed to be done differently the next time. We took stock of our current financial state and decided to register for the race at the earliest.

I tried to get in touch with both Chris O' Keefe and Alberto Blanco through Facebook. I wanted to better understand RAAM through their eyes. Alberto was a solo RAAM finisher, who finished as the best rookie of the race in 2011. He was also a professional bike racer before. Chris was also a solo RAAM finisher, who had vast ultra-cycling experience since 2005. With both of them on the team, I was able to get a very good perspective of the race. Both of them knew the race like the back of their hands. It was through them that I understood the importance of consistency in structured training, the importance of strong strategy, a strong crew, the vital role of nutrition and hydration, and having a strong sleep strategy.

I made up my mind to train under Alberto, who tried to understand me as a rider - my riding history, training time, the bicycles that I had, the nutrition, the crew and sponsors. He shared a training plan for the month of August 2017. I noticed the marked difference in the approach and style of training with Alberto, as he took into account all aspects of my day-to-day routine and my family life, and he made sure that training was top notch. The volume was around 15-20 hours a week and at a moderate intensity of around 17 mph. I could easily accommodate this training into my schedule, along with my routine job at the medical centre and still have time to spend with my family. The training was usually six days a week, twice a day during the weekday, and an eight-hour ride on Sundays. It never felt like a burden. I was very motivated to follow Alberto's training plan and gave him daily feedback on my performance. Alberto was always motivating me in whatever I did, never humiliated or showed doubts in me.

I also consulted with Chris O' Keefe to understand the preparations required in my approach to RAAM 2017. He suggested training under a coach, which Alberto was doing a spectacular job at. Chris is an experienced RAAM competitor when it comes to the race. He has done lot of Ultra-cycling races but remains very humble. Chris also shared his RAAM 2016 videos and stressed the importance of a strong sleep strategy and nutrition plan.

It was only a matter of time before I found myself on the registration page of the Race Across America 2017. I registered for the race by first week of August 2016 and requested Chris to be the Crew Chief. Chris took a weeks' time to decide on that and finally agreed to be the Team Leader of Team Srini for RAAM 2017. Chris wanted to understand everything that had happened with me in RAAM 2016, especially what went wrong, and then wanted to connect with the existing members of Team Srini.

L to R: Alberto Blanco (Coach) and Chris O Keefe (Crew Chief)

In the meantime, Sudhakara (Sudha), my friend from my school days, had reconnected with me on WhatsApp. We had lost touch in 1999, when Sudha went ahead to study Engineering and I went to Medical School. We had very rarely met from then onward, but were Facebook friends. Sudha had followed my Leh-Kanyakumari adventure and my RAAM 2016 race with great interest, and had also contributed to my crowdfunding campaign. He had strongly wished for me to finish RAAM 2016 and was really upset when I failed. When I did not finish in 2016, he intuitively knew that I would go back again and he told himself that if I did, he would support me on the front lines. Sudha sent me a Facebook message in July 2016, and I gave him a call immediately. We had a long chat about what had gone wrong in RAAM 2016. He responded, "Srini, I want you to finish RAAM successfully. Tell me, how can I help you?" I requested him to be a part of my crew for RAAM 2017.

He agreed. I had found a good friend coming back and supporting me, even though he did not have any idea what exactly he was getting himself into.

I contacted all my crew mates and convinced them to get on board. The cycle started all over again. By August 2016, I had Chris as Crew Chief, Prafulla, Dhana, Venky, Shreyas, and Sudha as crew members, and Alberto Blanco as my coach. In addition to this, Chris strongly felt that his sister-in-law Yin Shortland, who had crewed for him in RAAM 2016, would be a wonderful person to have on board. Subsequently, Chris and I approached her, and she agreed to crew for Team Srini. I felt quite confident with this experienced crew for my RAAM 2017 attempt.

I certainly did make use of my failure at RAAM 2016 for the better. I embraced it and believed in Kipling's words: "Unless you are in the pit, you never know the pleasure of reaching the summit." Failure helped me understand the race better. I now knew the importance of consistent training, sleep, nutrition and hydration, and a supportive crew. My respect for the race got bigger. As an individual, I focused on getting more grounded, more organized and humbler. Failure helped me to connect with people who had successfully completed RAAM in the past. I learnt to treasure the silver lining.

The race registration page on the RAAM website for RAAM 2017. Srini registers as early as July 2016

The race for me started in July 2016, on the day that I registered for RAAM 2017. It was almost 11 months prior to the race. The journey from then on was all about hours and hours of training, mileage running in thousands of kilometres, building a committed crew and planning the logistics. While training for RAAM, I had to leave my "normal" behind. No single day passed without talking about RAAM. It became my way of life. With relentless focus, I gave it everything it demanded, sacrificed the routine, controlled my thoughts and I trained consistently, and kept visualizing the finish line.

The striking difference between training for RAAM 2016 and RAAM 2017 was that this time, it did not feel like a burden in the slightest. My training was well adjusted with my busy schedule and family time. It was well balanced by Alberto. Prafulla felt good about the way I was training, and I could see that I was getting closer to my dream with each passing day. I believed in the process and believed I could do it.

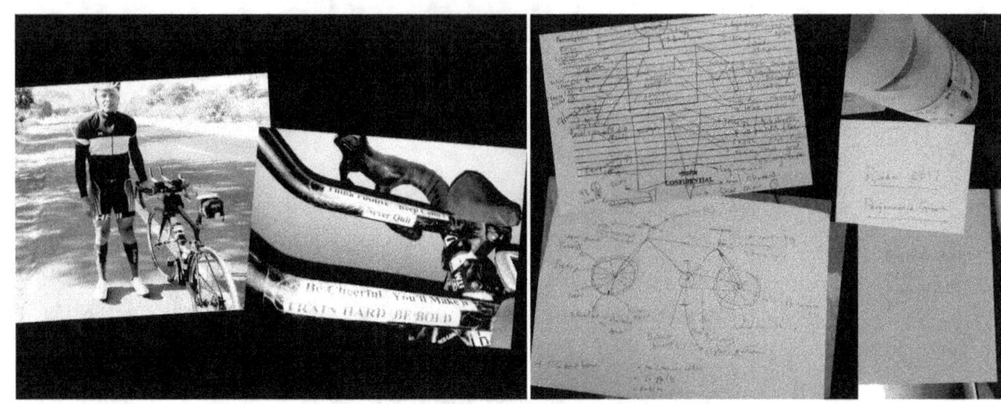

Planning and Training in Nashik along the Mumbai-Agra Highway

Srini with his family at Nashik in Sep 2016, L to R: Rohan, Prafulla and Srini

My desire to be the first Indian to finish this race had only grown stronger in all this time. The passwords to all my email and bank accounts had been set to "I will do it 2017 100%". It was this strong desire in me - exponentially larger than ever before, and only intensified by my experience of failure - that became a talisman that I found along this journey.

My intuition in reaching out to Chris and Alberto had served me immensely. Those brief but very powerful interactions had led to me finding the best Coach, Crew Chief and crew I could have asked for.

Chris conducted regular team meetings to brief the crew about the race strategy. His involvement for 11 months was intense with the clear objective of taking Team Srini to the finish line on time. Chris made all efforts to understand the strengths, weaknesses, likes and dislikes of me and the rest of the crew. He gave structure to the crew, brought in a lot of Organisational Behaviour; nothing was taken for granted. I, on the other hand, ensured that the roles of Crew Chief and Coach didn't collide, as I sensed a difference in opinion between Chris and Alberto quite early on. I made all efforts to avoid issues later. I involved my crew in major decision-making throughout the preparatory period.

By April 2017, Team Srini was set. There were four more crew members: - Supratim Pal, Rutvik khare, Maika Miller, and Sundaram Narayan on board. Alberto insisted that I should train in the US with him a month prior to the race, he asked me to plan out my itinerary accordingly. He lived in Seattle with his family. He wanted to physically prepare me in all aspects of the race even though we were geographically separated. I planned to go to Seattle by the first week of May, train for two weeks and then travel to Mountain View, California, where I would meet Chris, Yin, and Kishore, and then travel to

Oceanside, California for the race. The crew planned to join us at Oceanside by the first week of June. I had also worked out accommodation bookings at Camp Pendleton, Oceanside, and procured two support vans at Hertz.

I flew to Seattle with my bicycle to train with Alberto in the first week of May 2017. Prafulla prepared me to be independent and cook for myself for a month.

Srini travelling to Seattle at Mumbai Airport in May 2017

Alberto picked me up at the airport when I reached Seattle, Washington USA. He ensured that I trained peacefully while staying at his home. I met Alberto's wife, Veronica, and Miranda, his daughter. They were both very kind to me. I trained on the bicycle trails of Seattle and Alberto ensured I stayed safe and clocked in good training miles. He fine-tuned my riding with respect to the speeds that I have to ride in the race. Alberto also helped in getting my bicycles tuned for the race and briefed me on how to pace the race effectively.

Srini preparing for the first training ride in Seattle in May 2017

I carpooled my way to Mountain View, California, with some help from Kishore on finding a ride via Craig's list. I was travelling with an American lady who was moving out of Seattle with lock, stock, and barrel, so we were able to just about to fit my two bikes and three bags into her sedan. The 800-mile journey to Mountain View took us a little over 12 hours. When I offered to take over the wheel for a bit, she was not too comfortable with my driving, but I managed the night. Somewhere early in the morning, she took over the wheel once again and we started to chat about our lives. She admitted that she, too, was in two minds about sharing the ride, as was her family who was also sceptical about the idea of travelling with a stranger for 800 miles. She said she had felt safe during the journey, except for the few moments of panic when I drove the car. We reached Mountain View, California by mid-afternoon the next day and I stayed at Kishore's place. I finally met Chris, Yin Shortland and Anthony Shortland, (Yin's husband), who had strategized the race for Chris in RAAM 2016. He was the numbers guy. Anthony Shortland is Chris's brother-in-law. He had devised a mathematical model, a google spreadsheet that pegs the average speed and distance travelled by a rider in a given amount of time. All three datasets were logged onto a Google spreadsheet which would not only give the exact status of the ride, but could also predict the outcome of the race. The race plan is the key element in the race and the spreadsheet helped to know how the rider is performing with respect to the plan. This detailed spreadsheet mapped out target performances and also my actual performance during the race. The spreadsheet was prepared many weeks before the race. Anthony had come up with this model for Chris' race in 2016. He actually prototyped it on Chris's race in 2016 and he reset it to my race in 2017. Chris wanted Anthony's help with creating a similar model to monitor my progress in RAAM 2017.

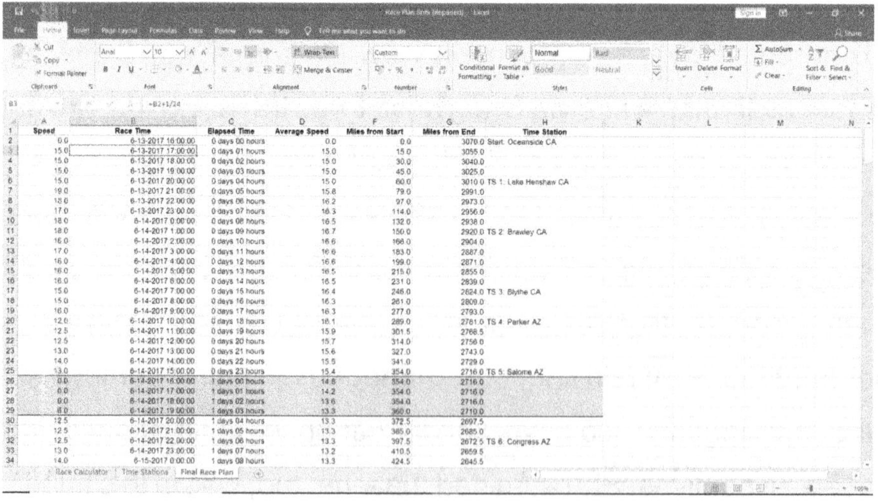

Speed	Race Time	Elapsed Time	Average Speed	Miles from Start	Miles from End	Time Station
0.0	6-13-2017 16:00:00	0 days 00 hours	0.0	0.0	3070.0	Start: Oceanside CA
15.0	6-13-2017 17:00:00	0 days 01 hours	15.0	15.0	3055.0	
15.0	6-13-2017 18:00:00	0 days 02 hours	15.0	30.0	3040.0	
15.0	6-13-2017 19:00:00	0 days 03 hours	15.0	45.0	3025.0	
15.0	6-13-2017 20:00:00	0 days 04 hours	15.0	60.0	3010.0	TS 1: Lake Henshaw CA
19.0	6-13-2017 21:00:00	0 days 05 hours	15.8	79.0	2991.0	
18.0	6-13-2017 22:00:00	0 days 06 hours	16.2	97.0	2973.0	
17.0	6-13-2017 23:00:00	0 days 07 hours	16.3	114.0	2956.0	
18.0	6-14-2017 0:00:00	0 days 08 hours	16.5	132.0	2938.0	
18.0	6-14-2017 1:00:00	0 days 09 hours	16.7	150.0	2920.0	TS 2: Brawley CA
16.0	6-14-2017 2:00:00	0 days 10 hours	16.6	166.0	2904.0	
17.0	6-14-2017 3:00:00	0 days 11 hours	16.6	183.0	2887.0	
16.0	6-14-2017 4:00:00	0 days 12 hours	16.6	199.0	2871.0	
16.0	6-14-2017 5:00:00	0 days 13 hours	16.5	215.0	2855.0	
16.0	6-14-2017 6:00:00	0 days 14 hours	16.5	231.0	2839.0	
15.0	6-14-2017 7:00:00	0 days 15 hours	16.4	246.0	2824.0	TS 3: Blythe CA
15.0	6-14-2017 8:00:00	0 days 16 hours	16.3	261.0	2809.0	
16.0	6-14-2017 9:00:00	0 days 17 hours	16.3	277.0	2793.0	
12.0	6-14-2017 10:00:00	0 days 18 hours	16.1	289.0	2781.0	TS 4: Parker AZ
12.5	6-14-2017 11:00:00	0 days 19 hours	15.9	301.5	2768.5	
12.5	6-14-2017 12:00:00	0 days 20 hours	15.7	314.0	2756.0	
13.0	6-14-2017 13:00:00	0 days 21 hours	15.6	327.0	2743.0	
14.0	6-14-2017 14:00:00	0 days 22 hours	15.5	341.0	2729.0	
13.0	6-14-2017 15:00:00	0 days 23 hours	15.4	354.0	2716.0	TS 5: Salome AZ
0.0	6-14-2017 16:00:00	1 days 00 hours	14.8	354.0	2716.0	
0.0	6-14-2017 17:00:00	1 days 01 hours	14.2	354.0	2716.0	
0.0	6-14-2017 18:00:00	1 days 02 hours	13.6	354.0	2716.0	
6.0	6-14-2017 19:00:00	1 days 03 hours	13.3	360.0	2710.0	
12.5	6-14-2017 20:00:00	1 days 04 hours	13.3	372.5	2697.5	
12.5	6-14-2017 21:00:00	1 days 05 hours	13.3	385.0	2685.0	
12.5	6-14-2017 22:00:00	1 days 06 hours	13.3	397.5	2672.5	TS 6: Congress AZ
13.0	6-14-2017 23:00:00	1 days 07 hours	13.2	410.5	2659.5	
14.0	6-15-2017 0:00:00	1 days 08 hours	13.3	424.5	2645.5	

Mathematical model created by Anthony Shortaland

Rutvik khare joined us at Mountain View. We did a couple of mock rides to dial in the communication equipment (Cardos/Terranos). He and I made our way to Oceanside, California, where we met Maika Miller, who guided us to the accommodations at Camp Pendleton. Maika worked as a security guard on contractual basis, and was supposed to crew for me in RAAM 2016, but could not make it. This time he would be part of our crew.

The next day, Rutvik and I picked up Sudha, Sundar, Prafulla, and Dhana from the Los Angeles Airport. As we arrived at Camp Pendleton, the whole crew was denied access to enter the camp for security reasons. We were detained at the entry gate for more than five hours for no valid reason, even though I had shared all the relevant email correspondences with the Camp Pendleton accommodation section. Finally, at midnight we were given access to the rooms.

The next day, I met the senior officers responsible for management and decided to withdraw the bookings. The security checks were tough on Team Srini's crew members. We checked out and decided to book two queen-sized rooms at the Quality Inn hotel run by an Indian-based company in the US. We finally moved into these rooms.

Prafulla discovered that she had left her kitchen box with condiments essential for the race at one of the rooms in Camp Pendleton. She insisted that it needed to be retrieved. Sudha and I made our way back to Camp Pendleton Once again, we were detained for three hours at the gate. We had to explain our reasons again; Sudha had to keep me from losing my cool. After much time and effort, we were able to retrieve our belongings and return to the inn.

That evening, I went on a mock ride with Sudha, Dhana, Sundar, and Rutvik as the crew in the follow-van. I maintained a steady pace till Lake

Henshaw. The mock ride went well and while returning from Lake Henshaw, they put me and my bicycle back in the car and each one of the crew members tried their hand at driving on the right side of the road, which is the norm in the US. Sudha and Rutvik were good drivers, but Sundar was not confident enough to drive.

Venky and Shreyas joined in later, while Chris and Yin drove from Mountain View, California to Oceanside the next day.

Three days before the race. On 11 June 2017, after almost 11 months, all the crew members were finally meeting one another in California. Chris had outlined the crew roles and crew shifts much in advance with no room for ambiguity. There was definitely a sense of familiarity amongst the crew and only minimal adjustments were required.

That morning, we had woken up to a wet morning drizzle which made the city weather quite pleasant. While the others were procuring our supplies from the supermarket, Shreyas, Venky, Sudhakara and Maika went to collect my racer-number and signage from the Race HQ. They picked up the racers' packet and took a snap of the racer line up.

Amit Samarth from Nagpur was one of the rookies in this race. Samim Rizvi from Bangalore had attempted RAAM thrice with no success or official finish and this was his fourth attempt at it. All three of us certainly had our eyes set on being the first Indian to finish Race across America.

So, who was it going to be? The race was on in another 48 hours. Remember Adam? He had been my Airbnb host last RAAM at Temecula, where me and my crew had stayed for a week. I had requested Adam to crew for this year's race, but due to some personal reasons he could not make it. Yet, he promised me that he would help us out with the logistics of the race.

I had had an issue with credit cards while renting the follow-van from Hertz. I sought Adam's help. The issue of a second follow vehicle was soon sorted. He also got us a camper stove with canisters and many US SIM cards for the crew to use. Prafulla, Venky, Shreyas and Dhana met Adam, Jennifer and his kids who had driven with him from Temecula to Oceanside. After a year we were all very happy to connect again. The rest of the day was spent preparing the vehicles with signage, setting up the bicycle rack and a 500w speaker on the roof of the follow vehicle. We had to be ready for the pre-race inspection and team debriefing the next day. Finally, the last crew member to join the party was Supratim, who was picked up from San Diego Airport.

Team Srini at Oceanside, California on 11 June 2017. L to R: 1ST row: Venky, Yin, Prafulla, Sudha, Dhana, Shreyas. L to R: 2nd row: Rutvik, Chris, Maika, Supratim, Sundar

Team Srini had two minivans which were rented and a small car which belonged to Chris O' Keefe. The minivans were being used for active follow and to run errands. The small car was our shuttle vehicle. Race officials were assigned to inspect these vehicles, the bicycles, and the race equipment. They also inspected the reflective tape on the bicycles, wheels and other safety gears. A detailed vehicle inspection of the headlights, parking lights, reverse lights, indicators, signage, slow moving vehicle triangle and caution stickers was also done.

That evening, Chris, Sudha and Shreyas attended the Crew chief meetings and joined me at the racers' meeting an hour later. As I sat at that briefing, a lot of things were running through my mind. I tried to control those thoughts by listening to Buddhist chants. Though I sat with my crew, I did not speak. I was trying to focus on the chants. I was soon introduced by the race media and joined the other racers on stage. Alberto was there to boost my morale and also had a word with the crew members to ensure this did not waver. The moments in that hall were pretty intense for me and my crew, partly because they now knew what kind of race they were dealing with! Later in the evening, Sudha gave a pep talk to me to give my best in the race and cautioned me to not to worry about unwanted things.

I slept at a different motel 15 minutes away from the crew that night. I was trying my best not to stress out instead I tried to visualize the journey and the finish line. I meditated before going to bed. I needed to calm my nerves. I hit the bed at 8:30 P.M. but still sleep eluded me. Chris briefed all the crew members on the tasks and challenges ahead.

13 Jun 2017 Race Day, RAAM 2017 Oceanside, California

I was up by 7:00 A.M. after a good night's sleep. I tried to pray, meditate, and do some free hand exercises. I had my breakfast by 8:00 A.M, and Sudha and Dhana arrived by 9:00 A.M, to meet me. Sudha spoke to me in Kannada, motivating me and drawing my focus to the essentials, and encouraging me to give all that I had toward this race. He reminded me of all the hardships that I had endured until this moment. He, too, wanted me to be the first Indian to finish Solo RAAM.

I put on my race gear and was ready for the show. Sudha stayed with me till 11:00. A.M, then drove me to the start line.

The support crew had prepared and packed their bags as planned earlier. They divided themselves into two teams; Day Crew and Night Crew. They had a quick team meeting, vehicle check, equipment checks before taking some time to relax; the calm before the storm. Chris was deep breathing to stay calm.

The crew hopped into their respective vehicles by 10:30. A.M. The Day Crew consisted of Yin, Venky, Sudhakara, Rutvik, and Prafulla. They took over the follow and errand vans. Shreyas, Chris, Supratim, Sundar, and Maika got into the shuttle car.

When our team arrived at the start line at the Oceanside Pier along the Pacific Ocean, the place was buzzing with RAAM racers and crew, support vans, fans of the race, bicycles and lights. The air sizzled with hopes, dreams and desires. The mood at Betsy's slot, the assembly point 200 m away from the start line, was frenzied.

Race Day: 13 June 2017, Betsy's slot with RAAM and RAW racers from different countries with their support vans and support crew

I kept my calm, still praying and listening to Buddhist chants in the follow van. By 12:00 P.M, I had lined up for my turn, although I still had another hour to go, before I launched. I sat with Yin, Prafulla, and Supratim till I was flagged off. With permanent RAAM racer number 558, I was due to flag off at 1:10 P.M.

8. DEEP HOLE

On 13 June 2017, at the start line of Race Across America 2017, I had a burning desire, sharp focus, supportive crew, and a strong strategy to make it to the finish line. RAAM is a unique roller coaster of a race with many ups and downs; not allowing any bit of mercy. It feels like sending a gladiator into a pit with a lion - looking death in the face is a part of it, and it is horrifying. This Race has a finite distance – 3089 miles and a finite time – 12 days or 288 hours. The race is inextricable, as staying on a knife edge for 12 days. The ability to finish is determined by the ability to deliver consistent performance on all these days.

Line up before the start of the race

3… 2… 1… "Go Srini Go!" Srini takes off at 1300 h on 13 June 2017 from the West Coast of America. Behind him is the support crew in the follow van

As always, they started calling the RAW (Race across the West, a 900-mile mini RAAM) solos first, then came the RAAM riders at around 1:00 pm. Finally, Race Director Rick Boethling and his father Fred Boethling, the CEO of the race called out, "The next rider is from India, Srinivas Gokulnath. This is his second attempt at the race after he did not finish in 2016, and this year he has Chris O' Keefe, a RAAM finisher, as his Crew Chief. He has trained under Alberto Blanco, who is also a RAAM finisher. India still awaits a solo RAAM finisher ..." The call came over the speakers and I made it to the starting line. I was calm and chanting the Tibetan Buddhist Chants, and visualising the finish line. I felt strong and in control of my thoughts. In fact, my mind had made vast space for this task ahead of time. 3 … 2 … 1 … Go!! I was on the move.

The start was fairly good and in comparison, to RAAM 2016, much more structured with a lot of purpose and commitment. The first 26 miles of the race course is the unsupported stretch. I was riding alongside the other Indian rider, Amit Samarth, and though we did not speak much, hand waves and thumbs-ups were frequently shared. I met my crew at the 26-mile mark. It was all smooth sailing till here. In the meantime, the Night Crew had left the scene at the starting point and Maika drove ahead taking the shortest route to Brawley, California, (Time Station 2) which is a small city on the race route about 145.4 miles from the start. As it was farming season, the city motels were full of Mexican workers with no vacant rooms at the first motel, but the night crew found a room with two beds, rested there and watched the live tracker. They waited out on the road to catch fast riders, like Marko Baloh and Sarah Cooper zooming past them.

I was sticking to the average speed as per the race strategy and reached the first Time Station, Lake Henshaw, at 16 mph. Before reaching Time Station 1, one of the race officials pointed out that the tail light or blinkers were not working on my bicycle. I tried to look around and pulled my left hamstring in that moment. This was quite a scare. But somehow, I managed to soft pedal and was out of the spasm in a few seconds. I was double checking on the reasons for the spasm. The crew did not notice it. As we reached Lake Henshaw, we saw a beautiful lake, but was more focused on getting to that famous descent of the RAAM course, the Glass Elevator. I proceeded with caution. The Glass Elevator is a 9% grade and some cyclists hit 60+ miles per hour on the descent. That thing is wicked! The descent is epic, as 50 miles into the race you enter the deserts of California, which is literally called a furnace; the ambient temperature being much hotter.

Soon after Christmas Circle, Srini's crew change the wheels on his bike along the race route. L to R: Prafulla, Dhana and Venky

The other half of the day crew, Yin, Sudha and Prafulla were waiting at Christmas Circle in an errand van. I needed a wheel and lights change, but nobody could find them. Yin and Sudha were frantically going through storage boxes in the back of the van, tossing things around while Prafulla was retrieving the wheel I needed. Panic was everywhere. I was pissed off. I felt they were taking too long, as such, a Type A guy like me make a big deal of nothing. Those few minutes, do they really matter? They finally found everything and changed the wheels on my bicycle to a faster, deep section variety. I was back on the road.

In the next few miles, I started to feel unwell. A bout of vomiting ensued, it was sudden and disturbing. I drank an Ensure (meal replacement drink) for a quick shot of vitamins and nutrients. In the next few miles, I started to feel unwell and a violent bout of vomiting ensued. It was sudden and disturbing. I drank some plain water, but had to stop briefly. Yin, Prafulla, and Venky were worried, of course. I asked Prafulla to give me an antiemetic tablet (Ondansetron + Pantoprazole). I gulped it down, but the nausea persisted. Better out than in! It felt better already, and I laid off the Ensure for a while.

I continued to pedal through the night with very minimal fluid intake. The crew did their best to hydrate me, but I was not very compliant to their instructions. They start introducing Ensure again but only a few sips at a time. It was better this time. Prafulla made me some chicken soup and porridge, which went down well. So, we carried on with the plain water and soup regimen that seemed to be working. Then we introduced sports gels, which are instant energy boosters that usually come in small palm-sized packs, with or without caffeine. These provide instant energy because of the high content of carbohydrates in them. I was much better hydrated by this point, managed a good wee, and it was clear!

The Day Crew were finishing their shift at midnight and we had reached Brawley, California (Time Station 2), where the Night Crew was waiting. The Night Crew was comprised of Crew Chief Chris O Keefe, Shreyas, Supratim, Sundar, and Maika. The day crew handed over the charge to the Night Crew, briefing them about me going low on fluid intake then headed off to Salome.

I had clocked a 16-miles/hr average by the second time station. The Night Crew's job was to get me to Salome, Arizona (Time Station 5) by the end of Day One. I had struggled between Parker, Arizona and Salome last year.

At the Mexican Border patrol between Brawley and Blythe, California, we were stopped for inspection by the United States Border Patrol and while the crew had their ID's handy, they forgot where they had kept mine in the car. This caused a few minutes of delay while Chris looked for it. Finally, Shreyas located it under the dashboard. We were granted permission to proceed.

Chris was in the follow vehicle along with Supratim and Shreyas, while Maika and Sundar were in the Errand Van. I was doing okay as per the strategy and Chris told me to go into cruise mode, and to keep drinking fluids.

The strategy was to feed me with 10,000 calories of liquid food in the form of Ensure oral nutrition (which is a rough equivalent of 20 McChicken Burgers or 50 samosas) and 20 litres of fluid every 24 hours for the next 12 days. Ultra-cycling races are huge battles of survival. When it comes to this kind of survival, it all boils down to the fundamentals, which are food, water, and sleep (khana, peena, sona). Discipline towards each one of them is the key. The hourly plan was to consume 350 calories of liquid food (Ensure) and 750 ml of electrolytes.

The first night of the race, I rode well, but ate poorly. I avoided Ensure and relied only on chicken soup. I rode toward the deserts of Arizona the next morning to Parker, Arizona (Time Station 4). The weather was getting hotter with temperatures soaring up to 110° F. The crew tried their best to contain me by keeping me drinking and hydrated and prevent me from getting a heat stroke. I was feeding although I was not faring too well. I was still avoiding Ensure as well as the Fast and Up electrolytes.

Riding as per the strategy, I reached Salome, Arizona by 12:30 P.M. The Day Crew had already earmarked the motel at which I took my first 3-hour sleep break. I did ok, but looked beaten. The Day Crew helped me get showered and fed me with some solid food. I struggled to sleep, kept waking up every now and then and finally after 2 hours I declared I couldn't sleep anymore. I also complained of a sore throat and asked Prafulla for an antibiotic. Yin instructed me to go to sleep and not to take antibiotic so early in the race, but I could not stick to her advice and wanted to get back on the bicycle. I also took the antibiotics.

The Support crew executed Day One as planned despite a few setbacks. The day ended at Time Station 5, 342.5 miles (550kms) into the race and averaging 14.5 mi/hour. At this point, Amit Samarth and Samim Rizvi, two other racers from India, were 30 and 65 miles behind me respectively.

Srini riding towards Salome, Arizona through the dry deserts

Day 2 (14 Jun 2017)

It was around 4:00 P.M.I was riding well to the next Time Station in Congress, Arizona (Time Station 6). The Day Crew was following me. At Congress, I spotted many solo racers hanging around, including Amit. I had two big climbs ahead of me - the Yarnelle Climb before Prescott (Time Station 7) and another climb before Camp Verde, Arizona (Time Station 8).

I was slowing down on the first climb and was overtaken by Amit. I did try to catch up but was unable to do so. I made it to Prescott, Arizona (Time Station 7) where my Night Crew took charge. Here, I saw Alberto, who was crewing for Joe Frank, another racer from USA.

After a brief pit stop, I rode towards Camp Verde, still slightly lagging behind as per the strategy, but with no red flags raised yet. Nutrition and hydration continued to be shoddy. We reached Camp Verde by 7:00 A.M. where I took another short break.

I was back on the bike and heading towards Flagstaff, Arizona (Time Station 9), 100 miles of an uphill stretch. I had bad memories of this stretch from RAAM 2016, and I was lagging behind, unable to ride any faster. I covered 30 miles in a little more than three hours. Chris was breaking his head, trying to figure out what was wrong with me. The plan was to roll to Flagstaff by the end of the night shift that marked Day 2 and let me have the scheduled sleep break.

The crew began looking for motels before Flagstaff. I was all beaten up. Yin managed to book a room at Happy Jack. It was the Day Crew's job to drive ahead of us and set up room, get the shower running, and crank up the air conditioner for the rider, but they weren't able to make it on time. The Night Crew decided not to stop at Happy Jack and instead kept pushing me 10 miles up the road. When the Day Crew caught up, they decided to put me to sleep in the van 40 miles behind Flagstaff. I hinted to Chris that I may have been dehydrated and needed intravenous fluid administered by my medic, Prafulla. Looking at my physical condition, it was decided to give me a bottle of IV while I slept. The Day Crew were also notified of my poor performance and condition.

Team Srini was in a deep hole.

Chris motivating Srini to ride stronger towards Flagstaff, Arizona.

At the start of the race, Chris found me to be strong, but by the second day he saw me struggling. One of the reasons was that my nutrition was way off from what had been planned. I did not stick to the plan and was wimpy about what was fed to me. Prafulla was especially worried about my condition.

Chris suggested some changes in the crew. Supratim was made the feeder with the Day Crew, and Sudha the feeder with the night crew.

Dhana was moved to the errand van from the follow van. Chris changed me up from the Fast and Up electrolyte to Skratch hydration. Skratch hydration mix is an American electrolyte replacement product which comes in powder form to be mixed in water, and it seemed to be better suited to the conditions of the American Continent. Chris instructed the feeders to meticulously log the intake. After three hours of sleep, I got back on the bicycle. I had around 40 miles to Flagstaff and was almost eight hours behind the schedule.

Srini with rider number 558 takes a sleep break 40 miles before reaching Flagstaff, Arizona

From then onward, the crew showed discipline in feeding and logging it in meticulously every hour. I was struggling, but pedalling to Flagstaff, reaching it by 7:30 P.M. Thereafter, I tried to ride faster on the downhill to Tuba City, Arizona (Time Station 10).

Before reaching Time Station 10, the Day Crew handed me over to the Night Crew, and Chris observed how well the Day Crew had done in feeding me, as per the strategy. I now rode to Tuba City and then towards Kayenta, Arizona (Time Station 11, the last time station in Arizona).

A few miles after Tuba City, I wanted to take a 10-minute power nap. When I got back on the bike, the Night Crew spiked me with coffee and started pushing me hard by blasting music on the speakers. I looked better and was coming back.

Before the start of the 20-mile descent I kept asking Shreyas the distance and how I was doing on Cardos/Terrano (the Bluetooth communication device used between rider and crew). Shreyas was blunt and said we were six hours behind schedule, and that if I wasn't focussed, we wouldn't make it to Durango, Colorado (Time Station 15 and the soft cut-off point). I did not want to hear that. Irritated, I replied, "I do not want to hear such negative things". Shreyas tossed the mike to Chris.

I was struggling to reach Kayenta. Chris was trying to motivate me to ride stronger. When we made it to Time Station 11 (Kayenta), I took a toilet break and got back on the bicycle. It was 9:30 A.M. The heat was on.

Chris calculated the numbers. There was an upcoming crew exchange 20 miles before Time Station 12, at Mexican Hat, Utah at around 2:00 P.M. The initial plan was to find a hotel at Montezuma Creek (Time Station 13), Utah. Now that was changed to Mexican Hat, Utah, one-time station behind where I was supposed to be as per the plan.

As I did the zombie ride towards Mexican Hat, Chris gave me the option of trying out the Spiz hydration powder. It still did not change my zombie riding, and I was losing time riding at this snails' pace. The Day Crew was almost crossing the Night Crew and the rider for a shift change.

In the meantime, I heard Chris say, "What the hell is this guy doing? I don't think he is going to make it to the finish line, or to Durango even! Have I signed up for a race where the racer is not prepared enough? He is not doing great; if he continues like this, I'm going to pack up my bags and go back".

9. THIS IS IT…

Srini takes a 2-hour sleep break at Hadrock Inn, Mexican Hat, Utah after the short intense meeting

Earlier, Chris had opined that the numbers were not looking bright, but magic could happen. I stuck to the strategy of taking a two-hour sleep break at Motel HadRock Inn at Mexican Hat. When I woke up from my sleep break, I had a very emotional conversation with Prafulla.

Prafulla asks me, "What is stopping you from riding stronger? Why can't you give your 100% when your crew is giving their time, energy, and resources for you to ride stronger? Do you have respect and regards towards the sacrifices made by your crew and family? What story will you tell back home? Will you tell people that you abandoned the race because you could ride only 12 miles per hour and not 14 miles per hour? What kind of example will you set for Rohan? Do you think we will be getting another chance? Do you understand the stakes involved?"

Tears rolled down both our faces. Prafulla told me to give my 100% and ride stronger till Durango. She told me not to overthink. I did not utter a single word, but got on the bicycle. The realization that so much was at stake, struck me deep within.

It was our "This is It" moment. Something had sparked within me and I was riding stronger, at 15 mph to Montezuma Creek (Time Station 13). I felt like I had to carry this race on my shoulders and take the whole of Team Srini to the finish line. The crew were amazed to see the difference in me. Dhana, Prafulla, Rutvik, Yin, Supratim, and Venky kept motivating me and cheered me on for the good work I was doing. The race took a turn and started to go well after that.

At the next time station in Cortez, Colorado (Time Station 14), the day crew handed over a stronger me to the Night Crew. My decision to make a change within me was amazing. The crew witnessed my transformation from being a rider who was riding very poorly to a rider who was more intense and showed the intent to ride stronger.

Srini riding stronger towards Cortez, Colorado with Dhana running and Cheering him

I was looking fresh when I arrived at Time Station 14. Without wasting any time, we swapped crews and continued towards Durango and the Rocky Mountains. Chris was motivating me; was impressed with my comeback. From then onward, he felt he should be in my corner of the ring and wanted to be the strong leader. He never wavered and stood strong with me.

We checked in at Time Station 15 in Durango, Colorado at 4:50 A.M. local time, 12 hours ahead of last years' time. I squeezed in a short 15-minute break. The crew spiked me up with some coffee and we continued towards Pagosa Springs, Colorado (Time Station 16).

Valerio Zamboni another solo racer from Monaco caught us on the climb and slowed down to say hello and patted on my back. Both of us were going back and forth for a while but eventually I got dropped as Valerio overtook me in that stretch.

10. TRANS STATE

Day five. Pagosa Springs - Alamosa.

The Day Crew had to chase me for over three hours in the morning to catch up with me. The Night Crew put me to sleep in the van on the side of the road before I attempted to climb Wolf Creek Pass. The Day Crew was late as they miscalculated the time and distance to marry up and Chris was frustrated. I woke up in an hour or so because I needed to pee, then went back to sleep for a little while longer. I got a massage and had something to eat. It was still not ideal since I hadn't had a solid three hours of sleep since the race had begun.

The Night Crew hopped into the shuttle, drove ahead for a quick stop at Wolf Creek pass, the "Continental Divide" and then found a hotel at Alamosa, Colorado (Time Station 18), where the next crew exchange was planned. When they got into the motel, they just did quick math and Anthony's spreadsheets showed us that I was nine hours behind the actual plan, but 15 hours ahead of last years' time. Sudha was frantically redoing the plan for the remainder of the race while Chris kept checking the Weather app, hoping conditions would be favourable later during the night.

Crew members motivating Srini with Graffiti on the road before Wolf Creek Pass

After my sleep break, I knew that I now had to cross the Wolf Creek pass, the highest point of the race at 10,000 ft altitude. I could see the snow-capped Rocky Mountains of Colorado, visible to me at almost a 20-mile distance. I had a close attachment to mountains as I had served in the high mountains between 14000 ft to 17500 ft for almost four years in India. I believe that they are divine and that they hold a lot of energy within. I felt the power within those mountains.

Looking at the mountain ranges, I told myself that I was not going to rush. Instead, I would gather all the energy from them as I pedalled amongst them. I wanted to be one with them.

I had to climb 10 miles to reach the summit of Wolf Creek Pass. Yin played battle march music as I entered a state of trance. I did not talk. I pedalled. It was like I was meditating on the bicycle. Supratim, Dhana, and Yin ran with me on the mountain. I slowly but consistently pedalled up the mountain. I was looking into myself, not saying a word, but feeding and drinking regularly.

We spotted another racer from Mexico behind us. I sharpened my focus till I reached the summit. Prafulla and Rutvik were already there, cheering for me. The climb, although slow, had gone well. As per my resolve during the ascent, I felt like I had gathered energy from the mountains and was able to later ride faster in the plains. The descent was smooth.

The Day Crew found a petrol station to fill up at, and I used the loo and jumped into a new pair of shorts.

Srini Climbing Wolf Creek pass, Colorado with Yin and Dhana cheering for him

I now had the plains of Colorado ahead of me, and wanted to make good time to the next Time Station in Alamosa (Time Station 18). I preferred my deep section wheels and rode faster that evening. Somewhere on this stretch, I was bitten by blood-sucking fleas, but reached Alamosa in good time.

The Day Crew were finishing their shift at midnight and were getting ready to hand me over to the night crew, but there were slight delays. As I continued to pedal, I encountered very strong headwinds. When the Day Crew was getting me geared up to get back on the bicycle after a short break, I wondered aloud how it would be so easy just to say, "Let's stop this, and not continue." I was exhausted at this point.

Yin talked to me. She told me to Let Go of all that I had on my mind. She encouraged me, saying that it was all about me and how I pedalled, and that there was no need to worry about the crew, about Prafulla, about cut-offs, about not making it, etc. I needed to mentally let it all go. She told me, "Yes it's a hard race, and it takes all your effort, but that's why we're here,"

Yin came up with our RAAM motto: "Bit by Bit" And though it is hard, it is okay to enjoy it. Forlorn at the end of the Day Shift, Yin was sad to see me this way. I was not happy with being on the bicycle, and adding to my exhaustion were the strong winds. It was dark and wild. I was weak and wanted some attention from my crew, which only Yin seemed to understand at that moment. I was seeking some kind of motivation. Perhaps the darkness and wind were adding to my melancholy. The extreme windy conditions prevailed as the Day Crew handed me over to the Night Crew. I did not want Yin to leave, but had to get on with the serious job in hand.

The support crew of Team Srini kept me entertained. The Day Crew was more calm, relaxed, and happy-go-lucky, the kind who would stop to take pictures and were always sweet and nice to me. It was fairly easy to keep your rider happy and moving while he was fresh. Yin had autonomy in the Day Crew. It was not what she asked for but it happened just by default. Her proactive initiatives and positive mindset at all times are the reasons.

The Day Crew kept reminding me, particularly Yin: "Bit by bit Srini, Race with Grace"

While the Night Crew was more serious and harder on me, as we hardly stopped to eat together and were always in a hurry, as if we were about to lose the race. They'd nearly beat up and push me close to the edge, but they were big mile-crunchers with Chris showering all kinds of motivational abuses on me.

The Night Crew would keep saying: "Go Srini Go!"

The crew model structured by Chris gave me a chance to look forward to a change every 12 hours. It was like 12 hours of extreme, nerve-wracking rock music when I was with the Night Crew and a calm, soothing music when I was with the Day Crew. I thoroughly enjoyed this combination of Yin (Day crew) and Yang (Night Crew).

11. WINDS, CHANTS & MOODS

Just when Team Srini thought things were getting better, Mother Nature decided to test us with strong winds, bone-chilling temperatures, and exhaustion in our souls. I was battling 26 mph headwinds, it was dark, cold, and daunting, but I kept fighting. The next time station, La Veta, Colorado (Time Station 19) was 50 miles/80 km ahead.

I was repeatedly being broken down due to the strong gusts of wind, and finally stopped. The Night Crew decided to put me inside the follow car and crank up the heater, while Shreyas fine-tuned the saddle position on the bicycle.

"What's happening, Sudha? Why am I not riding strong, what is happening with me?" I asked my crew member.

He listened patiently and advised me to put on the dove jacket, ski pants, and focus on my average speed. He cautioned me, as this would be the "Do or Die" moment of the race. He also said he would play the Buddhist chants from the follow van.

Chris sat silently in the co-driver's seat and was witnessing how I was dealing with the on-going crisis. Last year, I had gotten through this section of the race quite well and presumed it would be the same this time. But the winds were going crazy on me.

I got back on the bicycle. Sudha zipped up my Dove jacket and ski pants and the Buddhist chants started playing loud amidst the blowing winds. I particularly liked a chant called Barchey Lamsel which, as per Tibetan Buddhism, is the supplication to Guru Rinpoche for clearing the obstacles on one's path. It is considered to be the blessed words spoken by Padmasambhava before departing from Tibet. I first came in contact with Tibetan Buddhism in 2006 while serving at the Siachen Glacier with the Tibetan troops. In an effort to establish rapport with the troops then, I tried to learn their language and their prayers and would write them down in English. I found something special and divine in these mantras as I started to chant regularly. Eventually I also deciphered their meaning, and surprised the troops with the recital of these chants. I had spent around four months with the Tibetan troops and continued to recite the Buddhist prayers wherever I got posted to. I believed in their power; that reciting them could bring peace and harmony to the world.

At the present moment, I was on the bicycle listening to Barchey Lamsel, telling myself that I should stop worrying about the headwinds; these were things not in my control.   I should be focussing on my average speed and a good cadence on the bicycle. I understood one general concept during that ride through the headwinds: there is no point in worrying about things that are not in your control. Head winds, extremes of temperatures, rains, and high altitude. I can't control any of that. Problems need to be transformed into challenges. They need to be accepted and then worked on with a focus on the essentials.

I was cruising fairly well, despite inclement weather. Subtonic chants and prayers all have one thing in common - the healing frequency and the proven brain stimulation that I very much needed to fight the dark, cold, and windy conditions.

All of a sudden, I was telling my crew all about my Army posting at the Glacier and the influence it had on my life. In return, the crew kept assuring me that the winds would die as we went further down the route.

Strong head winds along the way towards La Veta pass. Srini fights it out!

In the meantime, Sudha, Chris, and Shreyas were constantly engaging me and talking about teamwork, self-belief and risk management. This change in my mindset worked in Team Srini's favour and I reached the La Veta Time Station. The crew was super stoked, motivated, and proud about how they had handled the crisis, believe me, it had the potential to derail the whole project of RAAM 2017.

Crossing La Veta pass, Colorado

Going from La Veta to Trinidad, Colorado (Time Station 20) and crossing the Cuchara Pass was the next task in hand. It was around 5:00 A.M., when I rode ahead from La Veta. The early morning light rays streaming on the grass combined with creek sounds and mule deer bucks in sight as we made our way to Cuchara, made this the prettiest of Colorado passes. I wished I could live there.

I went up the summit like a champ as Shreyas and Sudha took turns and ran alongside me on the 15-mile (24 km) climb. Things were falling into place, and I was no longer complaining about how long the climb was or what the distance left to the next time station was.

I was alive, truly alive!

Srini at the Summit of Cuchara Pass

The errand van with Maika and Sundar had to drive ahead to Trinidad, Colorado as their headlights needed a fix, but no automobile store was open that early so they joined the day crew and waited for the night crew at Time Station 20 in Trinidad, CO.

The Race Media crew had a chat with Chris before I reached Trinidad. It went live on Facebook. Chris said, "Srini is a fighter, a competitor, and he is coming back. I have never seen a guy who fights it out this way." I knew that Chris was back in the game and I was very glad to see him standing by my side.

The Team was in high spirits. I crushed the rest of the route and had a lot of fun doing it.

Chris's interview with the RAAM media before reaching Trinidad, Colorado. Chris was upbeat about the way Srini was riding.

The night crew rolled into Trinidad and handed me over to the hands of the Day Crew, who put me to bed. The Night Crew drove ahead to Springfield, Colorado, a deserted town in the heart of Middle America. The Night crew checked into Hotel Stage Stop that was run by an older couple.

Something had clicked! I looked very happy when the Day Crew received me. I was all smiles. I slept at the hotel, managing over two hours of sleep. I was getting better with the sleep schedule, but still not the ideal three hours.

As I rode through the Colorado plains, I felt motivated and happy to be on the bicycle after my sleep break. I learnt that all good could happen when I was riding stronger on the bicycle. I let myself loose to enjoy this process and was thinking free and was more relaxed than ever. I even came up with nicknames for the crew!

Venky and Yin cheering Srini between Trinidad, Colorado and Kim, Colorado

Chris- The Boss, Yin- The Master, Maika- Panda, Shreyas- Stud, Prafulla- Wife, Sudha- Friend, Dhana- The Rock, Supratim- The Secretary, Venky- The Velocraft, Rutvik- Street Smart, Sundar- The Lost, Chris D- RAAM Guru, Anthony Shortland- The numbers guy, Honey Badger- The RAAM Consultant.

My crew members while in active support, would cheer me with their own unique set of words to boost me up. Chris would be like most of the time, "You are killing it Dude". Shreyas would be shouting, "Go, Go, Go, keep the wheels rolling". Sudha, "Maga, come on maga! Don't give up!". Supratim, "Come on Man!". Yin, "Come on Srini! Bit by bit, race gracefully". Venky, "Doing good, Doing good Srini". Maika, "You got this man!". Dhana, "Super Sir, super!". These spirited words from my crew was keeping me strong all throughout the race.

Team Srini had the pleasure of three consultant-level members or advisors, outside the actual race: Anthony, Honey Badger (Martin Gruebele), and Chris Davies. Our three "outsider" consultants were not physically crewing but were dot-tracking my progress on the RAAM website and were providing regular inputs to my race. In RAAM, every rider on the race route can be tracked through a system that constantly updates time, location, current speed, and average speed. Our three "outsider" consultants were not physically crewing, but were dot tracking my progress on the RAAM website and were providing regular inputs to my race.

Anthony was watching all the numbers and logging in the current numbers into his mathematical model.

Martin Gruebele, also Called Honey Badger or HB (Head, Department of Chemistry Professor of Physics, Biophysics and Quantitative Biology, Illinois, USA). He finished RAAM solo in 2016 and he won his Age category (50 -59). HB is organised and a firm believer of regular sleep breaks in the race and thinks it is the key to success in RAAM.

Chris O keefe in 2016 finished second to HB. Chris was very impressed with the strategy which HB had. HB eventually even wrote a book on this strategy in the same year called Master's RAAM. Chris wanted me to follow the same sleep strategy as followed by HB. We followed the same strategy of sleeping three hours during the day and riding the bicycle for next 21 hours. I had never met HB or spoken to him, I had heard about HB through Chris and Chris was in constant communication with HB during RAAM 2017 on Facebook and on the phone.

Honey Badger was a McKinsey-level consultant in this race. He had even written a book on this race, and analysed the data and was providing constant feedback to Chris O Keefe. He is one of the foremost experts on the RAAM race.

Chris Davies was the RAAM Techie, who would give necessary information on winds, weather and other logistical challenges faced in the race. In RAAM 2016, he was the crew chief for Chris O' Keefe. Chris Davies from California was also in constant communication with Chris O' Keefe in my RAAM 2017.

All three consultants were like "500 USD an hour" for their time as they were our dream team of experts, and their presence proved to be undeniably invaluable.

I was, at long last, beginning to let go in the truest sense. The Day Crew played loud music for me since the Cardos communication system was no longer working and the crew could not talk to me. I was so overjoyed that I was dancing to the music on my bicycle!

12. SPARKED UP

I rode stronger to Kim, Colorado (Time Station 21), as the Day Crew drove me towards Walsh, Colorado. For the first time since the start of the race, the Night Crew had to chase their rider for a good 30 minutes, which was a good sign that I was riding strong.

I was in race mode as I entered the state of Kansas. I asked Chris for details about who topped the leader board for Ulysses, and rode even stronger so I could be in that Top 5. I averaged 16.5 mph to this time station. I got an hour's penalty for caravanning, that is when both the support vehicles were one behind the other at Montezuma Creek. The Day Crew had two follow vehicles in close proximity during active support that could have impeded traffic; hence, the race officials had issued a penalty. The crew decided not to tell me about this until 30 minutes before I reached Time Station 23 in Ulysses, Kansas. When I did find out, I took it casually.

The Night Crew made all the arrangements to put me to a quick nap while we served the penalty. The crew made use of the time to clean the bicycle in the light of the follow vehicle headlights; they wiped the frame, aero bars, wheels braking surface, cleaned chain, lube it up, and adjusted the brakes. They also decided to throw on a disc wheel, which could make me stronger.

After I was up and back on the road, the next time Station was at Montezuma, Kansas, around 50 miles away. For this time station, I actively tried to make it to the Top 3 of the leader board. Chris and the crew saw me in a different, "attack-mode" mindset, keeping my fatigue aside and focusing on excelling. Chris kept motivating me as we reached the Time Station 24 (Montezuma). I continued my momentum to TS 25, Greensburg, Kansas and clocked 16.3 mph. I was once again in the Top 3 of the leader board. The Night Crew followed me to Pratt, Kansas (Time Station 26), which is essentially the mid-point of the race at 1543 miles from the start and 1527 miles from the end. I clocked 16 mph and was in the Top 3 of the leader board. I then slowed down to Maize, Kansas (Time Station 27), but came back stronger again to El Dorado, Kansas (Time Station 28), and slept at a motel.

I rode with the Day Crew from El Dorado (Time Station 28) to Yates Center, Kansas (Time Station 29). I had been riding at a 10-mph average for the last five days and now rode 175 miles from Pratt to Yates Center in the 13 hours, delivering an average of 13.46 mph.

Now came the section from Yates Center (Time Station 29) to Fort Scott, Kansas (Time Station 30). This is the 60-mile section where I had suffered serious auditory and visual hallucinations during RAAM 2016. Those memories were lingering fresh on my mind. I remembered how bad I had suffered last year; I surely did not want to repeat that. It was 7:00 A.M.; I told myself I would ride strong.

I asked Chris about who heads the leader board and what was the top speed for this stretch. Chris said it was 19 mph by Patrick Gruner. I now had a target. I wanted to be on the Top 3 of that leader board.

I was thinking what could be the best thing that I could do for my crew and knew it would be to ride strong. I wanted to go above and beyond and give more than my 100% for this stretch, though I did not tell my crew. But these thoughts kept running in my mind. I let the monster out. I rode stronger, faster, and out of the saddle for almost 56 miles (90 km). Chris, Shreyas, and Sudha had never seen me ride this aggressively in the race. I kept roaring and talking to myself to push hard and give it all that I had. Even I was surprised to be in that zone. I continued this way for three more hours.

The Night Crew witnessed a spectacle on this stretch; they saw a crazy racer in their rider #558. I did not speak at all to my crew, for I was just hammering away at those pedals. I arrived at Fort Scott (Time Station 30) in style. I had clocked 17.3 mph and was second on the leader board, Strasser was third at 17 mph. Chris shared all this data with me and I was all the more motivated. Chris was very proud of the way I rode.

Srini riding strong the 70 mile stretch between Yates Centre, Kansas and Fort Scott, Kansas

Time station 30, Fort Scott is a special Time Station where the most famous RAAM fans, The Ashwill family were waiting to welcome Team Srini. Adam Ashwill was waving the Indian National Flag as I got there. I gave him a big hug and Chris told Adam that his racer had been riding like a champion. Later, Chris and I spent some 20 minutes at Ashwill's house. Chris asked me, "Dude, why did you ride like this, what made you ride like this?" I said, "I did this for you guys, for my crew, as that is the only best thing that I can give back for all the sacrifices which you guys are doing". This spark within me amazed the crew right from plains of

Colorado till now.

Chris was excited as he had not imagined that I would ride this fast topping the leader board, beating Christoph Strasser (six-time RAAM winner) in this section. Chris had tears of joy on witnessing this ride, which was unbelievable for those who were following Srini on the internet. The Night Crew took me out of Kansas and now we entered the state of Missouri. The Day Crew who were once again all set to receive me, 20 miles out of Fort Scott.

Srini welcomed by Adam Ashwill and his family at Fort Scott, Kansas

13. HUNGRY DEMON

20 Jun 2017, Weaubleau, Missouri (TS 31)

Day 8. Miles raced: 1844

The rolling terrain expanding over hundreds of kilometres is very unique to the state of Missouri. I could feel the momentum of the rollers welcoming a new Srini, who was ready to take on the race and was enjoying the ride as much as possible. I expressed this to Yin and Venky in the follow van. The Day Crew was happy to see their rider in this mood. I wanted them to play Tamil Kuthu songs, specifically "Madurai veeranthane" as I danced up and down the infinite rollers while still pedalling on that 60-mile stretch. I found a rhythm with the beats of the song and attacked the rolling terrain for the next two hours.

Team Srini reached Weaubleau and I wanted to know who all were ahead of me. Yin kept reminding me of the core principle of 'bit by bit', to be patient and to race gracefully. But I really did want to know where I stood in the race. The next Time Station 32 in Camdenton, Missouri was 50 miles ahead. I took four hours to get there, which was slow. The Day Crew decided to continue with me till Jefferson City, Missouri (TS 33).

My performance was a little lacklustre by now, so they plied me with food to have me energised. Venky thought I was slow because I had not eaten much before I went in for a sleep break. I don't know if this was really the cause. Of course, I was tired, but it was an incredibly hard race and I had pushed over the last couple of days. Chris called in and encouraged me, saying that where I was at with my current speed is fine. No need to kill it. This relaxed me. Then I chose my music to help me along, and I got into my groove again. At some point after Camdenton, Venky gave me information about where my next opponents were, especially as there was another Indian racer, Amit Samarth who also wanted to be the first Indian RAAM finisher. Amit was about 35 miles away.

Srini riding the rollers of Weaubleau, Missouri

This spurred me on, and I put in great work in attacking the rolling terrain to Jefferson City. I averaged 14.4 mph. The Day Crew saw me through to Jefferson City late past their shift, close to 3:00 A.M. I was very thankful to them for their support. They handed me over to the Night Crew at Jefferson City.

The night crew was upbeat and in race mode. Every time they got on board, there was a different spark in me. Chris got all the race updates to me and would make me livelier. He kept feeding data from Anthony Shortland who was keeping a very close watch on my race progress from California. Chris Davies was also constantly feeding information on being efficient in the race. When Chris O'Keefe shared communications from Martin Gruebele (Honey Badger), I was all excited to know what he feels about my race. The main reason for this is because Team Srini was following the same race strategy as devised by Martin Gruebele for his RAAM 2016.

There were also constant Facebook messages which Chris would read out. The resurgence of my place in the race was catching more eyes and hope for the dot trackers following Team Srini. Chris kept the heat on as far as Social media was concerned.

I was briefed about the progress we were making on the three riders who were ahead of me. I was crunching miles on each one of them. I was loving the race and the competition at this point.

We reached Time Station 34 in Washington, Missouri by 9:00 A.M. As we headed towards Time Station 35 which is the Mississippi River, I overtook Amit. By 30 hours into the start of this race, Amit had a lead of around 50 miles which increased to 100 miles by the 5th day. At TS 34, when I know I am not very far, there was some hope. But when I could see him right in front of me, things were getting real. Chris told me to keep a cool head.

Chris insisted me to talk to him and I asked, "How are you? Hope you are doing fine." Amit said he was okay; he had an upset stomach the previous night. I wished him good luck, Amit had a surprised look on his face, like, "Oh God! He is back", which was probably because Amit did not expect me closing the huge gap on him.

A brutally intense, hard core race to be the first Indian to finish RAAM began here at Missouri with more than 1200 miles of racing left to go. Team Srini had no intention of racing others to begin with, but it switched to intense racing to claim that coveted title. I kept riding ahead.

Srini overtaking Amit at Washington, Missouri

The night crew reached Time Station 35, the Mississippi River, well within the soft cut-off time, which I had failed to do last year. Everything was going well. On Day 9, I rolled into Alton (just after Mississippi river time station) to the Comfort Inn for my sleep break. I was tired, but happy that I had passed Amit. I managed to get a full three hours of sleep. For the shift handover the following night, the plan was to have a stop in Effingham, Illinois (Time Station 37) because the legendary Honey Badger was going to come down to meet me. But I was so fast, he didn't get there in time. So instead of stopping, I decided to ride ahead of Effingham. I spotted another solo racer Chris Hopkinson (Hoppo) from UK. I rode along with him and also had a brief chat. I raced ahead until we had to stop at the level crossing. This is where we changed shifts. In the next few minutes Amit also joined us at the level crossing waiting for the gates to open!

Srini riding side-by-side with Chris Hopkinson from UK at Effingham, Illinois

While in Effingham, my crew noted a peculiar race strategy of Amit; he was awakened from his sleep break by his crew members and family when they saw me zoom past the time station. They rushed a groggy Amit to get back on the bicycle and catch me. We understood that Amit's strategy was based on how I moved ahead in the course of the race, compromising on his sleep break. Team Srini ensured that we stuck to our strategy and no compromises would be made. After all, we believed in "Bit by bit, Race with Grace". Team Srini stuck to its principles.

The race evened out at the level crossing, where I was joined by Hoppo, and Amit. Hoppo and I greeted each other and Hoppo said I was doing really well and that I should keep going this way. I wished him good luck!

The Night Crew took over and I was in an aggressive race mode, but Yin was not happy with the kind of rush that I was into, she reminded me to "race with grace".

I had taken a considerable lead over Hoppo and Amit as I sailed through the next two-time stations Sullivan, (Time Station 38) and Bloomington, Indiana (Time Station 39). Before reaching Bloomington, I also overtook Joe Frank, for whom Alberto Blanco was the coach and crew chief. As I overtook Joe, I greeted him with a hand wave and was very excited to see Alberto after nine days on the race course. Alberto was generally happy for me. But in the next few minutes, Joe overtook me, yelled at me for nor rhyme or reason, and vanished ahead.

Chris watched the whole outburst and told me not to respond or lose my cool. I kept wondering as to why Joe was yelling. Chris said it happens in the race and to just ignore it. By the next mile, I overtook Joe silently. Joe rode up to me and apologised, and I told him not to worry about it and wished him luck. Later Joe also apologised to Chris.

Srini riding side-by-side with another solo racer Joe Frank from USA 40 miles before Bloomington, Indiana

At Bloomington, I met Dave Tanner, whom I had met the previous year and also at the start of RAAM 2017. I hadn't spoken to Dave for some time, but knew that Chris had spoken to him in a curt manner while we were in Mexican Hat. I was in an intense race and I didn't want to lose any momentum or time, so I merely shouted, "Thanks Dave, got to race, chat later!" I was moving fast, but still saw the spark in Dave's eyes. Feeling emotional, I stayed on the bike and flew towards the next time station.

The Night Crew handed me over to the Day Crew. I took a three-hour sleep break soon after Bloomington, even with Joe and Amit 15-20 miles ahead.

The weather turned bad with heavy rains that were coming from Hurricane Cindy. It was making life tougher for all racers and their crews.

I rode on to Greensburg, Indiana (Time Station 40). Time Station 40 was where Kishore had left the crew last year.

I rode stronger towards Oxford, Ohio (Time Station 41), a very special time station - it was the place where I had quit the race last year. I learnt from Prafulla and Rutvik, who were in the errand van of the Day Crew that Lisa Brunckhorst was waiting for Team Srini there. It was 11:00 P.M. when the crew in the follow van and I came into the time station. It was dark, but Lisa and her family members were shouting "Go Srini Go". I was holding great pace and felt bad that I could not stop, but Prafulla met Lisa and spoke to her and thanked her for her support.

It rained throughout the day, causing part of the RAAM route to flood and re-routing of the course. My crew had to stay on top of this. I didn't want to miss any turns or go down a wrong road. I maintained the lead and rode stronger through the rains to Blanchester (Time Station 42), Chillicothe (Time Station 43) and then Athens (Time Station 44), all in

Ohio. Before reaching Athens, I crashed into a pothole that was filled with water I survived what could have been a bad crash, checked on my collar bones and bicycle, and was relieved to see no breakage. The Night Crew helped me back on the bicycle. Chris told me to take it easy till we moved out of the city.

I continued to battle through rain and entered the state of West Virginia. Rains and hills with steep gradients all complicated the progress. I changed three sets of clothes in each crew shift.

We reached West Union, West Virginia (Time Station 45) and the night crew took over from there. Several unforced navigation errors happened before we reached the Grafton, West Virginia (Time Station 46) and McHenry, Maryland (Time Station 47) time stations. My lead that I had over Amit was diminishing. I was slowing down and he was catching up. I kept my cool and allowed the crew to rectify and proceed.

We reached McHenry, Maryland. I had covered 2800 miles and was left with 266 more miles to the finish line. I had around 30 hours left to make it to the finish. Since I was so tired, the Night Crew decided to give me a sleep break at 10:30 A.M. in the follow van at a fire station. Amit was just 10 miles behind me, but I went in for my last short two-hour sleep break.

Chris was in constant touch with Honey Badger, Chris Davies, and Anthony about this short sleep break decision. As I was sleeping in the follow van, the crew saw Amit pass. Sixty minutes later, they woke me up for the final battle.

14. THE LAST NIGHT

Yes, it was go time! "Go Srini Go!"

After the sleep break I had to cross the Appalachian Mountain Range. I was helped by my Day Crew, especially Dhana, who ran alongside me for a while. I crossed the mountain ranges at a constant pace and reached Cumberland, Maryland (Time Station 48). I was tired as I struggled to reach Hancock, Maryland (Time Station 49). I found company in another rider named Mark Gibson and tried to overtake him. Finding another racer on the race route is such a rarity in this long race and when you find one such racer, you are excited and want to be ahead of that racer. We saw each other many times before I overtook him it to Hancock.

The race was so close for Team Srini as we entered the Day 11. I was trailing behind Amit by around 15 miles which had the attention of many cycling enthusiasts from India and other countries

Chris slept very well that night. He had great confidence that I would finally make it. All these days had been very stressful for him with lots of doubts, emotions, and challenges being thrown at him. One important reason for Chris to sleep soundly was because of the positive feedback from all three RAAM consultants (Anthony, Honey Badger, and Chris D), especially Honey Badger who confidently told Chris O' Keefe that Amit was certainly not going to make it before Srini. He was as confident as making a casual observation about the weather, like, "Oh it's sunny outside." Honey Badger said to Chris, "Don't worry, you got this. It's no big deal, you're going to win; I guarantee it".

I rode forth with my Day Crew towards Rouzerville, Pennsylvania (Time Station 50). It was hilly terrain, but it still looked like everything was going to come down to the wire.

When I reached the Rouzerville time station, I spotted Amit ahead taking a sleep break in his follow van along the road. I waited for my Night Crew to takeover which took 20 minutes of the time and then we headed for the hunt. In the meantime, as soon as we reached Rouzerville, Amit started cycling and got a lead of 30 minutes.

The Day crew decided not to take their sleep break. They wanted to witness and support me on the last night of the race. I was not in great shape; I was groggy and tired. Chris sparked me up with coffee and a banana.

Srini climbing Appalachian mountain ranges and Dhana cheering him to ride stronger

I wanted to be the first Indian to finish RAAM in the solo category. I was ready to go for it and willing to put everything on the line. I rode stronger and brought out the monster within. That's when I spotted Amit's follow vehicle at a distance on an uphill. My target was locked in for the last night.

Although Chris did not expect Amit to be anywhere near me on the last day, Amit had taken a 30-minute cat nap. When his crew saw us right on their tail, they woke him up and put him on the bike.

I got closer and closer to my target and made a sprint. I overtook Amit. It was an easy task at that point. Sudha, Shreyas and I were all excited. The gas was on. It felt like the World Series was happening, or maybe the Super Bowl.

Team Srini passed him as if he was standing still--like in a movie. I felt like I was on a motorcycle rather than a bicycle. I was going fast!

Chris knew I was going to get him on this hill. Seeing this was a dream come true for Chris. He wanted me to knock Amit out exactly as I did.

I was off the saddle and riding hard. I had a mile over Amit in no time.

Amit's crew went into a panic mode; they kept going ahead of us to know how far the lead was.

We reached Time Station 51 in Hanover, Pennsylvania with an average speed of 14.3 mph and a 35 -minute, nine- mile lead over Amit. I had topped the leader board for Hanover Time Station and was not slowing down.

Once again, I beat Christoph Strasser for the TS 51 and was going great guns. The lead kept getting better and before the sun could rise on the last day of the race, I had a mighty lead of three hours.

Chris believed that I had a deep talent to dig deeper into my energy reserves. He had seen me in a crappy condition three hours back. Now he saw a different version of me. He saw a champion.

Chris had not seen anybody going from bad to good so quickly at the final stages of the race, where every racer was exhausted. Chris saw something unique in me.

Srini overtakes Amit and his follow vehicle between Rouzerville and Hancock on the last night of the race, establishing a significant lead

15. BREAKFAST AT ANNAPOLIS

Team Srini was cruising ahead, Sudha from the follow van told me, "Take us for lunch at Annapolis". I said I would take them to breakfast at Annapolis. I was very confident and in complete control.

The whole of Team Srini was on the road. We reached Mt Airy, Maryland (Time Station 52) by 7:00 A.M. We made a pit stop where Dhana gave me one final massage. All the crew members were chilled out by this point; they were relieved, and though exhausted, they were cheerful and full of life.

Chris was relaxing and making sure that there was no room for errors in navigation, and no rule violations. He kept telling the rider and the crew that our battle was not won until we crossed the finish line at Annapolis.

On the 40 mile stretch to Odenton, I kept riding strong, not slowing down, and keeping the lead at three hours at all times. Chris kept reading out the Facebook messages to me, which was a big morale boost. Sudha continued his meticulous feeding. The Day Crew were all along the race course cheering for me. Dhana was running on uphill by my side. It was a super, super fun mood. We reached Odenton, Maryland (Time Station 53) with an average speed of 13.3 mph.

Team Srini now had only 10 miles to the finish line. The Day Crew drove ahead to the finish line while the night crew followed me closely, making sure I was safe on the road. Chris had control over navigation with Shreyas driving the follow van. The errands van with Maika and Sundar had reached the finish line with the Day Crew.

The finish line was a saffron coloured, 2-inch-wide, 6 feet long line marking the end to a 3089-mile race. As I approached it, many emotions were flowing through me and my crew. Immense relief and a great feeling of accomplishment on one end of the spectrum; on the other, I was thinking about how I could express all the gratitude bursting through me towards my crew. There were no words.

As I crossed that finish line, joy and celebration exploded on the road. Team Srini was on top of the world. I got off the bicycle and hugged each of my crew members. They were emotional too, and not holding back their tears.

It was over now. I had become the first Indian to finish RAAM in the solo category.

Anthony video called me from California. I hugged the phone since he wasn't there to let me hug him in person. Kishore also spoke to me from California and was happy for me. It was the logical end to the unfinished business of RAAM 2016, of which Kishore had been an integral part. Maika played the Indian National Anthem soon after I had crossed the finish line and all crew members were very touched.

I was so relieved. There was so much space in my mind now. I felt the emotions that I experienced on the journey were much more intense than the ones I was experiencing presently, after crossing the finish line. Surprisingly, I was not crying - perhaps because I had cleared my tear glands while I was on the bicycle during the race. I had cried to myself while I was in the deep hole, while I was battling doubts and hopelessness, while Prafulla spoke to me in Mexican Hat, while climbing the high mountains of Colorado, while hit by with headwinds, while riding to Fort Scott and while the monster was let out on the last night of the race. So, here at the finish, I felt only peace.

Recap of Race Across America 2017

In this race, I suffered an intense dehydration issues as early as two days into the race. I was almost out of the race as I was seven hours behind the race plan at Flagstaff, Arizona (Time Station 9) and that just worsened exponentially as I went ahead in the race. At Mexican Hat, Utah (Time Station 11) I was 12 hours behind. At Ulysses, Kansas (Time station 21) I was 15 hours behind the race plan. I gradually pulled out from the deep hole with the help of my crew and began to start crunching miles. At Oxford, Ohio (Time Station 41), where I gave up in 2016 on the tenth day, this time I made it in 9 days 7 hours and was just 2 hours behind the race plan which we had devised. Finally, at the finish line I was 15 min ahead of the race plan.

I finished seventh in my category, having completed the race in 11days, 18 hours and 45 minutes. I was now escorted by the RAAM media van to the dockside finish at Annapolis. There was still a part of me that could not believe that I had finally finished RAAM, and I was thinking about my crew who sacrificed their time, energy and helped me get there. As I made my way to the big banner of the finish line podium, I got off my bicycle and bowed down to the finish line. Most racers lift their bicycles up overhead, but I bowed my head down with a feeling of submission, reverence, and thanksgiving.

And mostly, that wonderful feeling of LETTING GO…

Srini	Trinidad, CO, 1227.8 miles	Pratt, Kansas, 1606 miles	Camdenton, MO, 1893 miles	Greensburg, IN, 2403 miles	Finish Line, Annapolis, MD
Joe Frank	50 mi ahead	50 mi ahead	30 mi ahead	5 mi ahead	50 mi behind
Hoppo	60 mi ahead	60 mi ahead	40 mi ahead	50 mi behind	60 mi behind
Amit	60 mi ahead	100 mi ahead	35 mi ahead	30 mi behind	30 mi behind

Table: Srini was almost 60 miles behind the three racers Joe Frank, Hoppo and Amit at 1200 miles in the race. At 1600 miles, he was around 100 miles behind Amit. At 2400 miles he overtook Hoppo and Amit but Joe was 5 miles ahead. At the finish line, Srini had almost 30-60 miles lead over all three.

Team Srini on the finishers' podium of RAAM 2017 at Annapolis, Maryland on 25 June 2017. L to R: Venky, Yin, Shreyas, Dhana, Sundar, Chris, Srini, Prafulla, Maika, Sudha, Rutvik. Sitting: L to R: Supratim and Saran Preeti (race official)

I got on the podium to receive the finishers medal from the Executive Race Director Rick Boethling. The crew joined me with the Indian National Flag. I was later interviewed by George Thomas, the emcee for the finish line. George asked me, "How does it feel to be the first Indian to finish RAAM solo?" I told him I was very relieved. I told him about the relentless efforts behind this two-year long journey, and the sense of accomplishment at the present moment. George also asked "Were you and Amit racing to be the first finisher from India?" I said that since it was a race, me and my crew just gave everything we had to claim the title. I thanked my crew profusely and told George that without their selfless efforts, it would not have been possible to be at the finish line.

We clicked pictures and were due for our breakfast at Annapolis as I had promised. It was actually a brunch at a nearby American restaurant. For a moment, I felt so empty as for the first time in a long time, I had no goal, no deadlines and no targets to pursue. For the past 12 days, the focus had been on how to be better on the bike, and on accomplishing the set targets during the race. in fact, the last two years of my life had been all about getting to that finish line and the moment I was here, everything seemed to have come to a standstill. Almost like even if I die now, I'd be happy, no regrets! Strange, isn't it?

After our brunch, we headed to the hotel rooms, and incidentally our rooms were booked at the same place where the RAAM banquet for finishers was being held. I took a shower and shaved my beard for the evening. I put on my Hulk T-shirt for the occasion. It was lovely to see the crew all neat and smart for the banquet. I met Alberto at the banquet and thanked him for all he had done. I got my finishers' placard from George and had the opportunity to speak. I told everyone that RAAM had brought the monster out of me. I really had not planned to give a talk that evening, so it was brief then I joined my crew.

I still felt very empty in my thoughts. Supratim could not attend the banquet as he had to fly back to India the same evening from San Diego. Chris and Yin were also flying back to San Francisco soon after the banquet hall ceremony. The crew started to miss each other. It felt strange without the crew and without RAAM. Maika drove back the small car all the way back to the West Coast.

The strangest thing happened to me when I tried to sleep that night. I felt I was riding the bicycle, and it continued the whole night. Chris told me that it is natural and is called Ghost-riding, which would subside in a few weeks' time. I ended that marvellous day just ghost-riding all through the night.

The last team picture we took of RAAM 2017 at Annapolis, Maryland L to R: Yin, Maika, Rutvik, Prafulla, Srini, Dhana, Chris, Sudha, Shreyas, Sundar and Venky

16. LET GO

Even before the start of the race in 2016, I was consumed by everything happening around me. Apart from riding my bicycle, I was involved in the management aspects, documentation and other logistics issues of the team. I was trying to do all things at once, and was all over the place before the start of the race and this clouding of my mind continued all throughout the race. Not being able to Let Go and trust others with the roles that they had been assigned was one of the main reasons I lost focus during the race.

This continued even in RAAM 2017, but the intensity with which it happened was different. I did not know how to trust others completely. I was the kind of person who did not hesitate to convey my feelings of aversion towards lazy, lethargic people. I had no tolerance of it. I expected those around to think and act high and have big dreams. I found myself being impatient with those who didn't have the same high values or had fewer ambitions than me. But I've learned to accept that not everyone has the same priorities that I do. I had to learn to trust my crew. Every rider or team that has successfully completed RAAM will tell you that their success has everything to do with a good crew. After my failed attempt in 2016, I knew this, but I still had trouble letting go of my own need to control and micro-manage every aspect of this race and let my crew do their job.

In RAAM 2017, I was in a deep hole 72 hours into the race due to dehydration. The main reason for this dehydration was that I had not been feeding well with the right calories. I was so sissy about my calorie intake, in terms of I don't like that food, I want something else and not sticking to the plan. Each pedal stroke was getting harder, each up-slope on the road felt like a mountain. I didn't understand that I just needed regular calories in the simplest form to keep me alive in the race. My mind and body were not in sync. The strategy was well structured and laid out, but I had not surrendered myself to the crew, that is where the gap between my mind and body started to deepen. I had to learn to Let Go. I had to hand over my control to my crew. I had to eat what they gave me without complaining. I had to stop when they told me. I had to sleep when they told me. I was merely the man pedalling the bike, while they were my life support. My body was unable to ride stronger at around 30 hours into the race because of inadequate nutrition ;my mind did not want to accept that I was losing the race. I was still riding, but when I heard Chris say he had lost hope in me, I realized just how much trouble I was in.

It was a moment of destiny when I stopped the race and held an impromptu team meeting. We were in Utah. I was beaten up from the road, exhausted and upset. I wanted to take control of the situation, but learned that I couldn't. I needed to Let Go of that and let my crew do their jobs, if I wanted to finish this thing. I started listening to my crew members and finally surrendered to them. The race started to go right after that.

It wasn't long after the unplanned team meeting in RAAM 2017 when Prafulla questioned my intent to finish the race. She asked, "What is Stopping you from riding stronger, why can't you give it all when your crew can give 100%?". Although her tone was very assertive, it had a tinge of sadness in it. It did stir me up from within, I could not hold my emotions when she was talking. I patiently listened to her, I did not complain, I was not frustrated but was very open to appreciate her emotions towards the race. It was one of those, "this is it" moments. Intense as it is, the race forces into the rider a realization of all that is at stake, in a very short period of time, and also causes one to doubt one's capabilities in the face of such adversity. It is left to the rider to decide what to focus on. After that impassioned exchange with Prafulla, I consciously chose to Let Go of my apprehension as well as my comforts, and got on the bicycle with a burning desire to get to the finish line. This is how I improved my performance that year. I let go, and this ability of calculated disconnection from my negative beliefs at the right time was a necessary change in mindset. I could not let myself be consumed by my own fire. My monkey mind, never staying calm in one place, was a challenge to my progress and to my crew, but once it was tamed, the path to success became clearer.

Another prominent trait was my highly competitive nature; my need to excel even more in the presence of my competitors. The crew recognised that this trait was much like a demon waiting to burst out and they ensured that it was used to our advantage in the right moments, and was not to be expended casually. This quality was both a strength and a weakness, one that we optimised especially in my endeavour to be the first solo Indian RAAM finisher. I had to learn to trust others to do what's right. It wasn't an easy feat, but one well worth it.

Chris, too, had to Let Go of what was holding him back from expressing his honest opinion at Monument Valley in RAAM 2017, and that was an important turning point in the journey. Chris later (post-race) expressed that he did not have the courage to tell the truth when things were getting bad early in the race and it just poured out at that instant after 72 hours in the race. Although Chris never intended for me to hear his negative comments, he realizes that it set me off for the good. He feels that things don't always happen for a reason but this probably did, to end up well.

Parting conversations at the Dockside, Annapolis, Maryland L to R: Srini, Chris

Prafulla had to Let Go in many ways. Letting Rohan with her parents to crew for me in RAAM 2016 when I was struggling to find a crew was so difficult for her mother's heart. Meanwhile, she struggled to understand why I was not doing well. She Let Go her hesitancy to express herself to speak her mind during the race, then to insist we drive to the finish line to see how race finishers relish success. She also Let Go her spontaneous response and she replied Fred, "He is going to come back and be the first Indian to finish RAAM", when I was cornered by Fred's question, "Did You Get a Taste of RAAM?" in RAAM 2016.

In RAAM 2017, she Let Go her emotions at Mexican Hat when I was in the deep hole in the race and which eventually sparked me up to ride with intent. For the second time consecutively, she found the strength to, for a while, Let Go of Rohan.

Even my toddler son Rohan (Rohan) went through lot of sacrifice for my Ultra Cycling events. He was always clinging onto me for spending time with him. Rohan says "Papa! You can't go now; you need to play with me" whenever I am going out to ride. I felt bad for not giving my time to him then, questioning myself, what am I doing? Why am I doing? I tried my best explaining to Rohan that Papa needs to train to win the race. It was not convincing though. He wished I would stay home and play with him instead of going cycling. Earlier I used to come home for my lunch from office, following which I used to go for my training ride. Subsequently, I avoided going home for lunch to avoid Rohan feeling irritated about me going for cycling.

Prafulla and I decided to leave him with his grandparents in RAAM 2016 and 2017 knowing we would be gone for little over a month and that it would be stressful for him. Rohan was not completely weaned off and was still being breast fed in 2016 and 2017. It was a big challenge for Prafulla and her parents. Prafulla worked out all possible tantrum managing techniques to deal with Rohan's tantrums in her absence, right from toys, chocolates, cartoons and drives. She prepared her parents for all possible scenarios that they might come across. Both in RAAM 2016 & 2017, I left home a month prior to the race and Prafulla joined me two weeks before the race in USA. When I left home, there was not much of a cry but when Prafulla left home, Rohan was very upset and crying. Prafulla felt very sad about it but she managed by numbing herself with my desire to finish RAAM. Prafulla managed her absence by video calling Rohan as and when she found time, while she was not busy crewing. A toddler Letting Go of his parents for any period is very tough on the kid and his sacrifice is special for me.

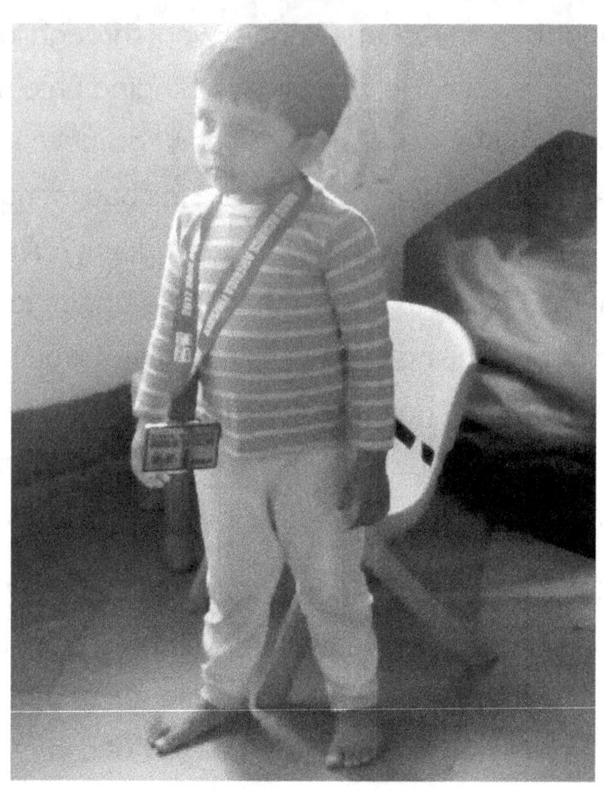

Rohan with the RAAM finishers medal in Nashik, Maharashtra

Sudha had to Let Go of his emotions right from September 2016 when he expressed his willingness to crew. During the race in 2017, Sudha didn't hesitate to speak his mind at all stages of the race, from the beginning till the end. When Chris had lost hope, Sudha tried to restore and rebuild it with his positive attitude.

All the crew members Let Go of their precious time, energy, comfort, hunger, sleep, family, and resources for me both in 2016 and 2017.

I began to appreciate the importance of "Letting Go" not just in RAAM. It has been an invaluable lesson that has been reinforced all throughout my life - from when I struggled to find admission to Grade 11 and had to Let Go of my casual attitude towards studies. I Let Go of my monkey brain, my ignorance, humiliation, ordinary routine, my disbelief in myself, my procrastination, weakness, my failure in RAAM 2016, my

144

stubbornness, my control-freak attitude, comfort zones, ego, and superficial predictive thinking. Let Go for me is a constant process of evolving and getting better. My story was an effort to emphasize the importance of this process, hoping that it will bring my reader more peace, success and prosperity.

"Let Go" works!

»»»

Srini continues to pursue his passion for Ultra-cycling, and participated in Race Around Austria in 2018. He has been serving as a United Nations Peacekeeper in South Sudan as of 2020.

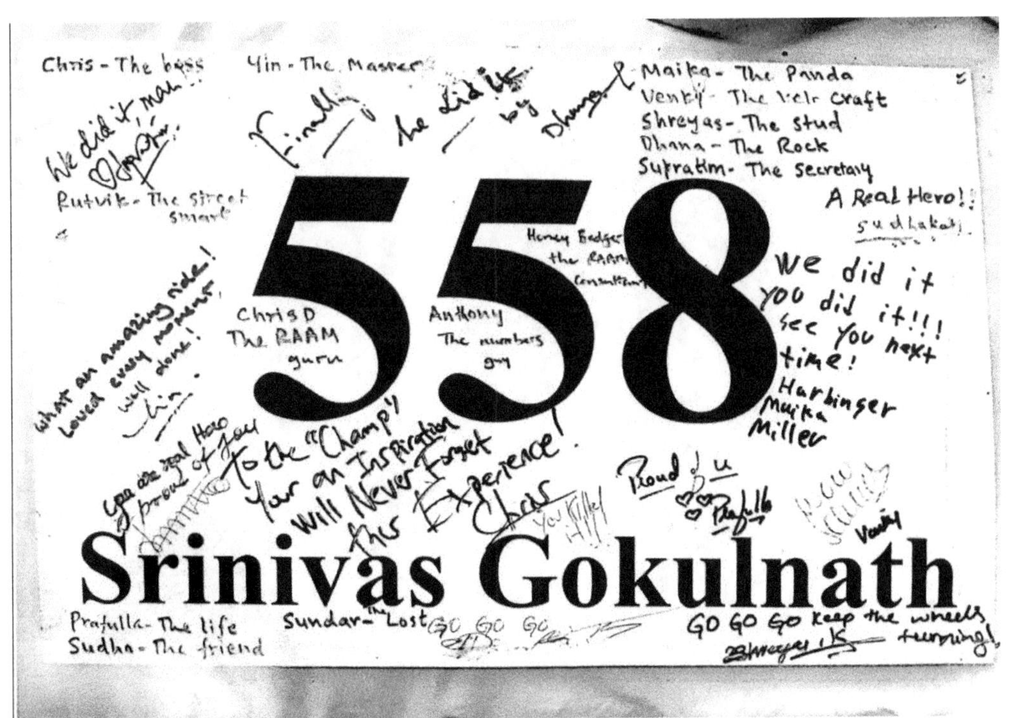

Race number 558 with the autographs of all crew members

www.ingramcontent.com/pod-product-compliance
Lightning Source LLC
Chambersburg PA
CBHW072234150726
48002CB00005B/2092